The Best of Andersen's Fairy Tales

Level 1
(1000-word)

Adapted by David Olivier

IBC パブリッシング

※本書はラダーシリーズ『アンデルセン珠玉童話選 (Andersen's Fairy Tales)』と
　『アンデルセン・クラシックス (Andersen's Classic Stories)』を元に再構成したものです。

はじめに

　ラダーシリーズは、「はしご（ladder）」を使って一歩一歩上を目指すように、学習者の実力に合わせ、無理なくステップアップできるよう開発された英文リーダーのシリーズです。

　リーディング力をつけるためには、繰り返したくさん読むこと、いわゆる「多読」がもっとも効果的な学習法であると言われています。多読では、「1. 速く 2. 訳さず英語のまま 3. なるべく辞書を使わず」に読むことが大切です。スピードを計るなど、速く読むよう心がけましょう（たとえばTOEIC®テストの音声スピードはおよそ1分間に150語です）。そして1語ずつ訳すのではなく、英語を英語のまま理解するくせをつけるようにします。こうして読み続けるうちに語感がついてきて、だんだんと英語が理解できるようになるのです。まずは、ラダーシリーズの中からあなたのレベルに合った本を選び、少しずつ英文に慣れ親しんでください。たくさんの本を手にとるうちに、英文書がすらすら読めるようになってくるはずです。

《本シリーズの特徴》
- 中学校レベルから中級者レベルまで5段階に分かれています。自分に合ったレベルからスタートしてください。
- クラシックから現代文学、ノンフィクション、ビジネスと幅広いジャンルを扱っています。あなたの興味に合わせてタイトルを選べます。
- 巻末のワードリストで、いつでもどこでも単語の意味を確認できます。レベル1、2では、文中の全ての単語が、レベル3以上は中学校レベル外の単語が掲載されています。
- カバーにヘッドホーンマークのついているタイトルは、オーディオ・サポートがあります。ウェブから購入／ダウンロードし、リスニング教材としても併用できます。

《使用語彙について》
レベル1：中学校で学習する単語約1000語

レベル2：レベル1の単語＋使用頻度の高い単語約300語

レベル3：レベル1の単語＋使用頻度の高い単語約600語

レベル4：レベル1の単語＋使用頻度の高い単語約1000語

レベル5：語彙制限なし

Contents

The Little Mermaid 1

The Emperor's New Clothes 55

The Steadfast Tin Soldier 69

The Ugly Duckling 83

Word List 106

The Little Mermaid

読みはじめる前に

The Little Mermaid で使われている用語です。わからない語は巻末のワードリストで確認しましょう。

- [ ] Sea-folk
- [ ] foam
- [ ] human
- [ ] immortal
- [ ] mankind
- [ ] oyster
- [ ] polypi
- [ ] soul
- [ ] storm
- [ ] toad
- [ ] willow

主な登場人物

Little mermaid　人魚姫　人魚の王の一番下の娘。人間の世界の王子に恋をしてしまう。

Prince　王子　人魚姫に命を助けられる。しかし、自分ではそのことを知らない。

Sea-princesses　人魚の姫たち　人魚姫の姉たち。人魚の王の娘は、15歳の誕生日になると、海の上の世界を見ることが許される。

Old grandmother　おばあさま　人魚姫たちの祖母。母親を亡くした彼女たちの面倒を見ている。

Sea-witch　人魚の魔法使い　暗い海の森の中に住んでいる魔法使い。人魚が人間のように2本足で歩くための方法を知っている。

Far out at sea the water is as blue as the loveliest blueflower and as clear as glass. But it is very deep—deeper than man can reach and deeper than many tall churches, one upon the other. Down there live people called the Sea-folk.

Please don't think that there is only white sand at the sea bottom. No, indeed! The most wonderful trees and plants grow there. Just a little movement of the water moves the leaves back and forth. The plants really look alive. And all the fish, big and small, swim among the branches just as the birds fly about the trees up here. In the deepest spot of all lies the Sea-King's palace. The walls and windows are made of beautiful sea plants and the tops of shells. These shells are lovely. In every one there lies a large, shining pearl.

The Sea-King's wife had died many years ago, so his aged mother took care of his house. She was a wise woman. She was also proud of the family she was born into. She was an important person among the Sea-folk, so she wore twelve oysters on her tail. The other important folk could only wear six. Most folk thought highly of her; especially because she took loving care of the little Sea-princesses, her granddaughters. They were six pretty girls, but the youngest one was the loveliest of them all. Her skin was the color of a rose leaf, and her eyes were as blue as the deepest sea. But, like the others, she had no feet. Her body ended in a fish's tail.

All day long they used to play in the

palace's great rooms. There, the living flowers grew upon the walls. When the tall windows were opened, the fish would swim in; just as birds fly into our homes when we open the windows. The fish would swim up to the little princesses and eat from their hands.

Around the palace was a large garden full of bright red and dark blue trees; the fruit shined like gold, and the flowers like burning fire. The soil itself was the finest blue sand. Everything had a bluish color. One might think that one was up in the sky rather than at the bottom of the sea. And when the sea was still, one could see the sun; it looked like a bright, red flower.

Each of the little princesses had her own garden where she could plant as she pleased. One princess gave her flower-place the form of a large fish; another the form of a mermaid. But the youngest planted hers in a circle to look like the sun. She used only the reddest of flowers. She was an unusual child, quiet and thoughtful. Her sisters liked to fill their gardens with strange things from sunken ships. But, beside her sunny flowers, she had only a pretty statue of a handsome boy. It was made of white marble which she found on a sunken ship. Next to this statue she planted a tree with long leaves. It is called a willow tree. The willow's leaves waved back and forth nearly touching the soil.

Her greatest joy was to hear about the world of mankind above. She made her old grandmother tell her about ships and towns, people and animals. She thought it was especially wonderful that the flowers on earth could be smelled; they cannot be smelled at the bottom of the sea. Also, that the woods were green and that the fishes in the branches could sing loudly and beautifully. It was the birds, you see, that her grandmother called fishes. Her granddaughters had never seen birds, and, therefore, couldn't understand.

"When you reach your fifteenth birthday," said the grandmother, "you may rise up out of the sea. You may sit in the moonshine on the rocks and see the big ships sail by. Forests and cities you shall also see."

In the following year, the oldest sister would become fifteen; but how about the others? Each girl was one year younger than the next, so the youngest would have to wait five whole years. Then she too could come up and see what our world is like. But each sister promised to tell the others what she saw and what she enjoyed the most. There were many things their grandmother did not tell them which they wanted to know.

But it was the youngest girl who wanted to know more than the others. She also had the longest time to wait. Often she stood at the open window and looked up through the dark blue water. Beyond the swimming fish she could see the moon and stars. They were not so bright, of course, but they were there. When something like a dark cloud passed overhead, she knew it was either a large fish or a ship with many people. Certainly the people on board the ship never dreamed that a pretty mermaid stood below looking up at them.

And now the oldest princess was fifteen years old and able to rise to the surface of the sea. When she came back she had hundreds of things to tell her sisters. But the nicest thing of all, she said, was to lie in the moonshine on a sandbank. From there by the shore she could see the large town and its many lights. The lights looked like stars. She could also hear the noises of busy people and of bells ringing in their churches. She had a strong desire to go on shore. But she knew she could not.

Oh, how the younger sister listened! And afterwards, she stood in the evening at the open window. She looked up through the water and thought of the great city with all its people and noise. She even thought she heard the church bells ringing.

The next year the second sister was allowed to rise to the surface. She too could swim anywhere she wanted. She went up just as the sun was going down. And she thought the sunset was the prettiest sight of all. The whole sky looked like gold, she said; and the beauty of the clouds was beyond words. Red, orange and pink, they sailed over her head. But faster than the clouds was a group of wild ducks flying in front of the sun. She also swam towards the sun, but it sank into the sea before she could get to it.

A year after that the third sister came up to the surface. She had no fear, so she swam up a broad river from the sea. She saw pretty green hills covered with fruit trees; castles and country houses hidden by the lovely woods; she heard the birds singing; and the bright sun made her face burn. In a small stream she came across lots of children. They were running around with no clothes and playing in the water. She wanted to play with them. But when they saw her they became afraid and ran away. Soon, a little black animal began shouting at her. It was a dog, but she had never seen a dog before. Then she became afraid and swam back to the open sea. But never could she forget the lovely woods, the green hills and the pretty children—the children who could swim in the water without fish tails.

The fourth sister did not go near the shore. Instead, she stayed out in the middle of the sea and said that was the nicest of all. One could see for miles and miles around, and the sky looked like a large glass bell. She had seen ships too, but far away. She saw fish called dolphins, which could jump high into the air. And the largest creatures in the sea, called whales, blew water up through their noses.

Then it was the turn of the fifth sister. Her birthday was in the winter. She saw what the others had not seen their first times. The sea had quite a green color with very large, white ice mountains floating about. Each looked like a pearl, she said.

They had the strangest forms and shone like diamonds. She sat on one of the largest ice mountains and watched the ships pass by. The ships all seemed very afraid of the ice. In the evening, the sky became cloudy and stormy. She enjoyed the wind blowing her long hair. All the ships took down their sails. She could see the fear in the sailors' eyes as they passed near the giant ice mountain. Yet she sat quietly in the middle of the troubled sea.

The first time each of the sisters rose to the surface was always a new and wondrous experience. All of them were surprised by the beautiful things they saw. Later, however, when they could go above anytime they wanted, they were no longer very interested. After that first time, they didn't care so much about the world above. They longed to stay in the deep water. It was nicest down below at home, they said.

Often in the evenings the five sisters would hold hands and rise in a row to the water's surface. All of them had beautiful voices, sweeter than any human's. When a storm was blowing and they thought a ship might sink, they would swim in front of the ship. Then they would sing sweetly to the sailors. They told the sailors of the beautiful world under the sea, and not to be afraid to come down. But the sailors couldn't understand their words. They thought the voices came from the wind. Nor did the sailors ever see the beautiful Sea-King's palace; for the men were always dead when their bodies reached the sea bottom.

Now when the sisters rose together to the surface, the little sister would stand and watch them from the window. She felt sad and alone and wanted to cry. But mermaids have no tears and so they suffer even more.

"Oh, I wish I were fifteen!" said she. "I know that I shall love the world above and the men who live there."

And at last she became fifteen years old.

"Well, now we don't have to worry about you anymore," said her grandmother. "Come here and let me dress you like your sisters." And she placed a hat of white sea flowers in her hair. Then the old lady tied eight large oysters to the Princess' tail. Everyone would know she was an important mermaid.

"But they hurt me so!" said the little mermaid.

"Yes, but sometimes we must suffer for the right appearances," said her grandmother.

Oh, how glad the little mermaid would have been not to wear these fine things. She liked the red flowers from her garden much better. But she didn't dare take them off. "Goodbye!" she said and rose lightly up to the surface.

The sun had just set when she raised her head above the water. The clouds were pink and gold. In the middle of the sky shined the evening star, clear and lovely. The air was cool and fair, the sea like glass.

A large black ship with three masts lay nearby. Only one sail was up because there was no wind. Many sailors could be seen on the ship, and music and singing could be heard. As the evening grew dark hundreds of pretty lights were lit on board. The little mermaid swam close to the ship. Every time the water raised her up she would look into the ship's window. She saw many well-dressed people. The handsomest was surely a young Prince with large black eyes. He looked to be about sixteen years old at the most. Just like the little mermaid, this was his birthday too. The ship was the scene of his birthday party. On board, the sailors were dancing. When the Prince came out from inside, many rockets were shot into the air. For a moment the night looked like day. The little mermaid became a little afraid and swam under the water. But soon she came up again to look. It seemed as if all the stars from heaven were falling down on her. She had never

seen such fireworks. Large suns turned in fast circles, throwing off fiery colors. And the flat, quiet sea was like a mirror in which you could see everything. It was so bright on the ship that you could see every face clearly. Oh, how handsome the young Prince looked. He was laughing and smiling and shaking hands while the music continued into the night.

It grew late, but the little mermaid could not take her eyes from the ship and the handsome Prince. Now the lights and the fireworks were put out, and things were quieter. But from deep down in the sea there came a low sound. It seemed to grow louder. Still, she rested on the surface, moving up and down with the water and looking into the ship's window. Then the ship began to move faster as the sailors raised the sails. From far away she could see the lightning from a storm.

And a fearful storm it was. The large ship rolled up and down on the angry ocean. The water rose like great black mountains and looked as if it might cover the ship. But the ship was like a duck and it floated on top of the water. The little mermaid was enjoying the show, but the sailors were not. Then, as wave after wave hit the poor ship, it began to come apart. First one piece of wood then another started to break. The ship turned on its side and the water rushed in. Now the little mermaid saw that they were in danger. She had to watch out for all the pieces of broken ship now in the water. For a moment it was quite dark and she could see nothing. Then in the lightning of the storm she could see everyone falling and rolling into the water. She looked especially for the young Prince and saw him sinking into the deep sea. This made her happy because now he would come to visit her. But then she realized that human beings cannot live under water; he would die before he reached her father's palace. Oh no! He must not die. So she swam among the pieces of ship looking for him. She seemed to forget the danger that she was in. She ducked below the water and came up again next to him. He had no more power in his arms and legs, and his eyes were closed. Surely he would have died if the little mermaid had not saved him. She held his head above the water, and let the waves take them away.

When morning came the storm had passed. There was nothing left of the ship. The sun rose red from the water. The Prince's face regained some color but his eyes were still closed. The mermaid kissed his handsome forehead and pulled back his hair. He looked just like the statue down in her little garden. She kissed him again and longed that he might live.

And now in front of her she saw land. The high, snowy mountains looking like beautiful clouds. Near the shore were lovely green forests. In front stood a white building. It looked like a church. Lemon and orange trees grew in the garden. At that point there was a small bay; the shore had fine white sand. She swam there with the handsome Prince and laid him on the sand. She made sure that his head was higher than his body in the warm sunshine.

And now the bells in the white building started ringing. A number of girls then came walking through the garden. The little mermaid swam out behind some high rocks in the water so that none could see her. There she watched to see who would come to the poor Prince.

It wasn't long before a young girl walked by. At first, she was afraid when she saw him; but only for a moment. Then she ran to find some other people. The little mermaid could see the Prince come to life again. He smiled at the girl and those around him. But he did not smile at the mermaid, because of course he didn't know that she saved him. When they carried him away into a large building she felt very sad. She swam down under the water and returned to her father's palace.

She was always more quiet and thoughtful than her sisters but after this she became even more so. When her sisters asked her what she had seen when she went above for the first time, she told them nothing.

On many mornings and evenings she rose to the spot where she had last seen the Prince. She saw how the fruits on the trees grew large and were then picked; she saw how the snow turned to water on the high mountains, but she did not see the Prince. Every time she returned home sadder and sadder. The only thing she enjoyed doing was sitting in her little garden. There, she would put her arms around the pretty statue that looked like the Prince. But she did not take care of her flowers at all. They began to grow long and wild—over the walkways and through the branches and leaves of the trees. Soon it became quite dark and sad under their shade.

At last her sadness became too much for her, so she told her story to one of her sisters. Soon the other sisters and several friends also heard it. One of these friends happened to know who the Prince was and everything about him. She had also seen the party on board the ship. She knew where he came from and where his kingdom was.

"Come, little sister!" said the other Princesses. Arm in arm, they all rose in a long row up to the surface. They went to where they knew the Prince's palace stood. It was built of a light, yellow, shining stone. It had wide, marble steps, one of which reached down to the sea. There were beautiful statues all around the building, and lovely gardens and walls. There were high windows that you could look through to see large paintings on the walls. In the middle of the largest room was a big fountain; the water from the fountain went high in the air towards the glass roof and came down again.

So now she knew where the Prince lived.

On many evenings she rose from the sea and swam near his palace; much nearer than the others dared. In fact, she swam up the little palace waterway to a place under the marble wall. Here she used to sit and watch the young Prince, who thought he was alone in the bright moonshine.

Many an evening she saw him sail in his beautiful boat, with music playing. She would watch from behind the green sea plants. Sometimes the wind would catch and blow her silvery hair. When people saw that they thought it was the wings of a lovely white bird.

Many a night, too, she would listen to the fishermen talk while they worked. They spoke very highly of the young Prince and said only good things about him. She was happier than ever that she had saved his life. And she remembered his head resting on her breast and how she had kissed him. But since he knew nothing of this, he could not even dream about her. More and more she began to love mankind.

More and more she wanted to be among people. Their world seemed so much greater than her own. They could fly across the sea in ships; go up to the highest mountains; and their land of trees and fields continued farther than her eye could see.

She wanted to know much more. She asked her sisters, but they were not able to answer her questions. So she asked her grandmother, who knew much about the upper world.

"If men do not get drowned," asked the little mermaid, "can they live forever? Don't they die like we do down here in the sea?

"Yes," said the old lady, "they also must die. In fact, their lives are shorter than ours. We can live to be three hundred years old. But when we die, we disappear forever, like foam upon the water. We do not have immortal souls; we never enter into a new life. We are like the green sea rushes—if they are cut down, they cannot grow again. But men are different. They have souls which always live—even after the body is lying in the earth. They rise up through the clear air to the shining stars. As we rise out of the sea to the land of men, so men's souls rise to beautiful unknown places which we will never know."

"Why do we not have an immortal soul?" asked the little mermaid sadly. "I would gladly give my hundreds of years to be a human being for a single day; then I might hope to live in the world above the sky!"

"You must not trouble yourself about that," said the grandmother. "We have a much better and happier life than mankind above."

"So I shall die and disappear like foam? Hear no more music of the sea? No more pretty flowers and red sun? You mean there is nothing I can do to win an immortal soul?"

"There is!" said the old grandmother. "Only if a man grew to love you more dearly than anything else in the world. If he loved you with all his heart and soul; and if, before a priest, you both promised to be true for now and forever, then his soul would become yours. Only then could you share that happiness that comes to human beings. He would have given you a soul, and yet kept his own. But that can never be! We are different from them. A thing of beauty like your fish's tail is thought to be ugly by people; because they know no better. Up there one must have two strange things called legs to be thought handsome!"

Then the little mermaid looked sadly at her fish's tail.

"We should be happy the way we are," said the old lady, "and really enjoy the three hundred years we have to live. I'm telling you we have a nice long time. Why don't we have a Court dance this very evening!"

Indeed it was a beautiful sight, one that you would never see on earth. The walls of the large dance hall were of clear, thick glass. Hundreds of giant green and red sea shells were hanging on both sides. Bright blue lights made the room shine through the walls and into the sea around. Countless fish of all sizes and colors swam by to look.

Through the great ballroom ran a broad stream; on this the mermen and mermaids danced to their own pretty songs. Such lovely voices are unknown on earth. The little mermaid's voice was the sweetest of all. For a moment her heart was glad. She knew she had the prettiest voice of all living things—on the earth or in the sea. But soon her thoughts turned back to the world above her. She couldn't forget the handsome Prince, nor could she forget that she didn't have, like him, an immortal soul. So she left her father's palace during the party and sat sadly in her garden.

Here she heard the sound of a ship's bell coming down through the water. "I know he is sailing up above—he whom I love more than my mother or father: he to whom my heart wants to belong. I will do everything I can to win him and an immortal soul! While my sisters are dancing in the palace, I will go to the Sea-witch. I have always been afraid of her before, but maybe now she can help me," she thought.

So the little mermaid swam out of her part of the sea. She swam towards the dangerous turning water where the Sea-witch lived. She'd never been there before. No flowers or sea plants grew there; only the cold, gray sea bottom. Then she saw the turning water which pulled down everything near it into the deep. On the other side was where the Sea-witch lived. The witch's home was in a very strange forest; a forest of tree snakes—half animal, half plant—called polypi. These terrible things tried to catch and hold anything that came near. She could see the bones of fish, humans, and even another mermaid in these polypi. She had to swim through them and the turning water to reach the Sea-witch's house. She became very afraid and wanted to go home. But then she thought of the Prince, and her strength came back. She tied her hair so that the polypi could not catch it. Then she crossed her arms and swam as fast as she could. She did it!

Now she came to a large, dirty and dark place in the woods. Here were fat, ugly water-snakes floating around. In the middle of this space was a house. It was built from the bones of sailors. Here sat the Sea-witch; a toad was eating from her mouth; the fat water-snakes were moving around her body.

"I know what you want!" said the Sea-witch; "you are a foolish girl! But you shall have your own way, for you will get into trouble, my pretty Princess. You no longer want your fish's tail, eh? You want to walk around on legs like men, do you, so that the young Prince will fall in love with you? You want him and an immortal soul at the same time!"

Then the witch let out a fearfully loud laugh; the toad and the snakes fell to the ground.

"You have come at the right time," said the witch; "If you had come tomorrow, I couldn't have helped you for another year. I will make you a magic drink. Then you must swim to land, sit on the shore and drink all of it before sunrise. Then your tail will become two nice legs. But it will hurt; it will feel like a sword is cutting you in half. Those who see you will say you are the loveliest girl alive. You will be able to walk and dance beautifully; but every step will feel painful. If you want to suffer all this, I have the power to help you."

"I do," said the little mermaid, her voice shaking; she thought of the Prince and of having an immortal soul.

"But remember," said the witch, "once you have a human form you can never become a mermaid again! You will never be able to dive down through the water to your father's palace. And if you fail to win the Prince's love—his love for you above all things—then you will not gain an immortal soul. The morning after he marries another, your heart will break: And your body will become like foam upon the water."

"So be it!" said the little mermaid, but she was so afraid.

"You must pay me too," said the witch, "and it will not be a small thing that I demand. You have the loveliest voice of all things here at the bottom of the sea. You believe you can win the Prince with that voice, I know. But no, you must give that voice to me. I want to have the finest part of you in return for my magic drink. For in my magic drink I must include my own blood."

"But if you take my voice," asked the little mermaid, "what will I have left?"

"Your lovely body," said the witch, "your light walk and your speaking eyes. I think you can fool a man's heart with those. Well! Do you have the nerve? Put out your little tongue and I will cut it off as payment; and you shall have the magic drink!"

"All right, then!" said the little mermaid. The witch started a fire to make her magic drink. "A clean pot is best," she said. Then she picked up two or three snakes and used them to clean the pot. After that, she cut open her own breast and her black blood dropped into the pot. Every moment she added something fresh into the pot. Soon it was quite hot; the sounds were loud and the smells were strong. At last, when the drink was ready, it looked like the clearest water!

"Here you are!" said the witch. Then she cut out the tongue of the little mermaid. Now the mermaid could not speak at all; nor could she sing.

"If the polypi touch you on your way out," said the witch, "just throw one drop of this magic drink on them. It will kill them!" But the little mermaid didn't need to do this. When the polypi saw the magic drink in her hand, they backed away in fear. Very soon she passed through the forest and the dangerous turning water.

She could see her father's palace. The lights in the long dance hall were off; everyone inside was sleeping. But she dared not visit them, now that she couldn't speak. Now she was going to leave them forever. Her heart felt as if it might break in two. She entered the garden and picked a flower from each of her sister's flower beds. Then she threw a thousand kisses towards the palace and rose through the dark waters.

She arrived at the Prince's palace shortly before the sun rose. She went to the marble steps and sat down. Then she drank the magic drink. It felt as though a two-sided sword was cutting through her body. She was in great pain and lay there like a dead person.

When the sun came over the sea she woke up. The pain was very sharp but in front of her stood the handsome young Prince. He looked at her with his dark eyes for a long time; finally, she looked down and noticed that her fish tail had become pretty white legs. But she was wearing no clothes and covered herself with her long, thick hair. The Prince asked who she was and how she got there. But she could only look at him with her dark blue eyes, for she couldn't speak. Then he took her by the hand and led her into the palace. As the witch said, every step was like walking on sword points. But she accepted the pain.

Hand in hand they walked along, while others watched them. They were surprised at her beauty and light, floating movements.

Now she was dressed in the most costly silk clothes. None in the palace was as lovely as her. But she could neither sing nor speak. Other young ladies, dressed in gold and silk, came and sang to the Prince and his parents. One of them sang more sweetly than the others. The Prince seemed quite happy. This troubled the little mermaid, for she knew that her voice was far prettier, and she thought: "Oh, that he might know the truth—that I have given away my voice forever to be near him!"

Then the other girls danced some light and pretty dances to lovely music. At this the little mermaid stood up. She lifted her lovely white arms and began to float across the floor as none other had done before. Every moment made her beauty more clear. Her eyes also spoke more deeply to the heart than the songs of the other girls.

Everyone came to like her, especially the Prince. She danced more and more; though each step she took was very painful. The Prince declared that she should always be with him. She was allowed to sit outside his door.

Presently, he had her dressed in men's clothing so that she might ride horses with him. They rode together through the pretty-smelling woods; where green branches touched their shoulders and little birds sang among the fresh green leaves. She also walked right up the high mountains with him. Although blood came from her feet, she only tried to laugh at her suffering. She followed him higher until they could see the clouds floating like birds below them.

At night, while others slept in the Prince's palace, she would walk out on the broad marble steps. For it cooled her burning feet to stand in the cold sea water. She thought of her family and friends far below in the water.

One night her sisters rose up arm in arm. They sang so sadly as they swam in the water. They saw each other. Her sisters then told her how sad she had made them by leaving.

After that, they visited her every night. Once, a long way off, she saw her aged grandmother; she had not come to the surface for many years. She also saw her father, the Sea-King. They held out their hands to her but dared not come so close to land as her sisters.

Every day she became dearer to the Prince. He loved her as one might love a dear, good child; but he never thought about making her his wife. Yet his wife she must become; if not she would disappear like the foam on the morning after he married another.

"Do you love me most of all?" the eyes of the mermaid seemed to ask him when he kissed her forehead.

"Yes, you are dearest of all to me," said the Prince, "for you have the best heart. You are the kindest to me. You are like a lovely young lady I once saw but shall never see again. I was on a ship that sunk in a storm. The waves brought me ashore near a holy temple, where many young girls were studying. The youngest, who found me on the shore and saved my life, I only saw twice. She is the only one I could love in this world; but you are like her. You almost make me forget her. She belongs to the holy temple; therefore, my good fortune has sent you to me instead, and we will never part."

"Alas! He does not know that it was I who saved his life," thought the little mermaid. "I carried him across the sea to the wood where the holy temple stands. I sat behind the rocks and watched to see if anyone would come. I saw the pretty girl that he loves more than he does me!" The mermaid wanted to cry but she could not. "He says the girl belongs to that holy temple, and will never come out into the world; and they will never meet again. I am with him; I see him every day. I will love him and give my life to him!"

But now there was talk that the Prince was to marry. They said he was to take the lovely daughter of the neighboring king to be his wife. That's why he was now preparing to sail away on a fine ship. "The Prince is traveling to see the land of the neighboring king," they said; but everyone knew he was really going to see the king's daughter.

The little mermaid shook her head and smiled. She knew the Prince's thoughts better than the others. "I must travel," he said to her. "I must see this beautiful Princess because my parents want me to; but they shall not force me to marry her. I cannot love her; she is not like the lovely girl in the temple whom you are like. Should I ever choose a bride, I would rather have you, my speechless lovely!" And he kissed her mouth, played with her long hair, and laid his head close to her heart. She dreamed of human happiness and an immortal soul.

"Surely you are not afraid of the sea, my speechless child!" said he. They were standing together on the fine ship carrying him to the land of the neighboring king. And he talked to her of the sea, of nice days and stormy ones, of the strange fish in the deep and what is down there. She smiled, for she knew better than any human about the bottom of the sea.

In the moonlight, when all on board were asleep, she sat at the side of the ship and looked down through the clear water. She seemed to see her father's palace. High above it stood the old grandmother with her silver crown on her head; she was looking up at the ship's bottom. Then her sisters came up to the surface. They looked at her sadly and moved towards her. She smiled, and would have told them she was well and happy, but a sailor came by just then.

Her sisters dived below the waves, and she was no longer sure that she had really seen them.

The next morning the ship sailed into the neighboring king's city. The church bells were ringing; flags flew from the tops of buildings, and the king's soldiers stood holding their shining swords.

Every day brought a large dinner with music and dancing. But the Princess was not yet there. She was being brought up in a holy temple far away, they said. There she was learning things that a good Princess should know. At last she arrived.

Like others, the little mermaid really wanted to see her loveliness. And it was true; a more beautiful face she had never seen. Her skin, her hair, and her dark blue eyes were like those of a goddess.

"It is you!" cried the Prince, "you who

saved me when I lay on the sea-shore!" And he held his bride-to-be. "Oh! I am so happy, I don't know what to do!" he said to the mermaid. "My greatest wish has come true. You too will share my happiness, for you love me more than all of them!" And the little mermaid kissed his hand, but already she felt her heart would break. Yes, the morning after his wedding would mean her death.

All the bells were ringing and word of their wedding was passing through the city. All the preparations were made in the church. The bride and bridegroom stood before the priest and received his holy words. The little mermaid was dressed in cloth of gold. She stood behind the bride and held her dress. But her ears did not hear the wedding music, nor did her eyes really see the wedding. She thought of her night of death, of all that she lost in this world.

The same evening, the bride and bridegroom went aboard the ship. Guns were fired, flags were waved, and a special bridal room and bed were prepared.

The sails opened up in the light wind, and the ship floated lightly over the ocean. When it became dark, colored lights were lit. The sailors danced happily on board. The little mermaid thought of the first time she had risen above the sea. Then she had seen the same partying. And she danced for them; round and round she turned, floating along the deck like a bird. Never had she danced so beautifully. As always, there was the pain of sharp sword points in her feet, but she didn't think about it. Instead, the pain in her heart was far worse. She knew that this was the last time she would see him; the Prince for whom she had given up her voice, her family and home, and suffered such pain every day. And still he could know nothing of it. This would be the last time she would look at the sea and the stars. Forever after this she would see nothing, for she had no soul and could not get one.

All was joyful on board the ship until after midnight. She danced and laughed with the others but thought of death in her heart. The Prince kissed his lovely bride, and she played with his black hair. Arm in arm they went to rest in their beautiful room.

Later, all was still and dark on board. The little mermaid rested on the side of the ship looking east to where the sun would rise. The first light, she knew, must kill her. Then she saw her sisters rise from the sea. They looked as white as she. Their long fair hair no longer blew in the wind; it had all been cut off.

"We have given it to the Sea-witch so that you may not die tonight! She has given us this small sword! Before the sun rises you must push this sword into the Prince's heart; Then, when his warm blood touches your feet, they will again become a fish's tail and you will once more be a mermaid. Then you may come back to us and live your three hundred years before you die. Please hurry! Either he or you must die before sunrise. Our old grandmother has become so sad that her hair has fallen out; ours has been cut off by the witch. Kill the Prince and come back to us! Hurry! Don't you see the red lines in the sky far away? A few more minutes and the rising sun will kill you." And they sank again beneath the waves.

The little mermaid quietly opened the door to the Prince's room. She saw the beautiful bride asleep with her head on the Prince's breast. She walked to the bed, stood over the Prince, and kissed him while he slept. Then she looked up at the sky which was becoming redder and redder. She then looked at the sword in her hand, and again at the Prince. The Prince, in his dreams, called his bride by name; she alone was in his thoughts. The mermaid's hand was shaking. Should she strike? Another moment passed and she threw the sword far away into the waves. They became red where it fell, as if the sea was bleeding. Once again she looked with painful eyes at the Prince. Then she jumped from the ship into the sea, and felt her body changing into foam.

And now the sun rose out of the sea. Its heat fell with gentle warmth upon the cold sea foam, and the little mermaid did not feel the touch of death. She saw the bright sun. Above her were hundreds of beautiful forms with no bodies. They were floating in the air. She could still see the white sails of the ship and the red clouds in the sky.

The voices of the forms were musical; but so heavenly that no human ear could hear them. Nor could any human eye see them. They had no wings but floated in the air because they were so light.

The little mermaid now had a body like theirs. It rose higher and higher from out of the foam.

"To whom have I come?" she cried. Her voice sounded like that of the other beings. It was so heavenly that no earthly music could equal it.

"To the daughters of the air," they answered; "a mermaid does not have an immortal soul, and can never have one unless she win's a man's love. Her after-life is decided by a power beyond her.

"The daughters of the air have no immortal souls either, but they can get one by their good acts.

"We fly to the hot countries where the heat and sickness destroy men's children. There we bring coolness and the smell of flowers to make people happy and healthy.

"After we have tried to do such good things for three hundred years, we can have an immortal soul like human beings. You, poor little mermaid, have tried to do good with all your heart. Like us, you have suffered and become a child of the air. Therefore, you too can win an immortal soul for yourself with three hundred years of good acts."

The little mermaid raised her bright arms to the sun. For the first time she felt tears in her eyes.

On board the ship a new day was beginning. She saw the Prince and his beautiful bride looking for her. They were watching the foam on the waves as if they knew she had jumped to her death.

Unseen by either of them, she kissed the bride's forehead and smiled upon the Prince. Then she rose with the other children of the air up to the clouds which were sailing the sky.

"For three hundred years we shall float and float and float. One day we will float right into God's kingdom."

"Yes, and we may get there still sooner," one said softly. "Unseen we enter the houses of men where there are children. When we find a good child who makes happy his parent's hearts, then God shortens the time of our efforts. The child does not know when we fly through the room; but when we smile with joy at such a child, a whole year is taken from the three hundred.

"But whenever we see a bad or mean child we cry tears of sadness. And every tear adds a day to our efforts!"

The Emperor's New Clothes

読みはじめる前に

The Emperor's New Clothes で使われている用語です。
わからない語は巻末のワードリストで確認しましょう。

- [ ] pretender
- [ ] march
- [ ] unfit
- [ ] minister
- [ ] able
- [ ] empty

用語解説

The Grand Procession 大行列　王が家臣を連れて街を練り歩く行事。

coat 上着　外套だけでなく背広もcoatと言う。

loom 織り機

material 材料、素材　ここでは洋服を作る「生地」のこと。

pants ズボン　「下着」のときは、underwear ／ underpantsのように言う。

pattern 模様　洋服の柄や模様のこと。

stockings 靴下　男性用の長い靴下のこと。

主な登場人物

Emperor 皇帝　洋服が大好きで、特別な服を作る織り手がいると聞き、ぜひ服を作ってもらいたいと考える。

Weaver 織り手　「愚かな人、今の仕事に向いていない人には見えない」特別な服を作るというふれこみでやってくる。

Old minister 老臣　有能なことで知られる家臣。服を見ることができず、思わずウソをついてしまう。

Many years ago, there lived an Emperor who loved new clothes. He spent most of his money on buying these fine, new clothes. He cared about nothing else, really. Not his army, not the arts, not even his people. No, he just liked to show off his new clothes. He had a different coat for every day of the year, and every hour of the day. In many countries, kings and emperors are busy with important matters. But this Emperor was usually busy changing his clothes.

The Emperor lived in a large, pleasant city. Every day, many strangers would come to the city for business or pleasure. One day, two men who said they were weavers arrived in the Emperor's city. They said they could weave the most beautiful and colorful clothes in the world. They used only the finest material. They also said that the clothes they made were very, very special. These clothes could not be seen by foolish people or by people who were unfit for their jobs. However, nobody knew that these men were not really weavers. They were only pretenders.

When the Emperor heard of these men he was very interested. "These clothes would be of great value to me," thought the Emperor. "By wearing them I would know who was foolish and who was not. I would also know which of my ministers was unfit for his office. Yes, I want to wear some of that special cloth at once." He then gave the two men a lot of money in advance to begin their work.

So the men set up two weaving machines, called looms, and pretended to weave. But of course, there was nothing on the looms. They demanded the highest priced silk and gold materials. They put these materials in a safe place. Then they pretended to work on the empty looms until late at night.

"I wonder how my new clothes are coming along," thought the Emperor, after two days had passed. In his heart, he was a little afraid to visit the weavers. Because he remembered that foolish or unfit people could not see the cloth. Of course, he did not believe that he himself was foolish or unfit. He just thought it might be a good idea to send someone else first. "I will send my able old minister to check on the clothes," thought the Emperor. "For he is wise and surely fit for his office."

By now, most people in the city had heard of the wonderful new cloth. Everyone wanted to see how foolish or unfit their neighbors were. "The old minister also knew of the cloth. When he walked into the room he saw the two men working at an empty loom. "Oh my!" he thought and opened his eyes very wide. "I can't see anything." But he was careful not to say so.

The two pretenders asked him to come closer. They asked him if he thought the colors were beautiful. They pointed to the looms. The poor old minister looked hard but couldn't see a thing. Because there was nothing to see. "Oh my!" thought the minister. "Is it possible I am foolish? Or unfit for my office? I never thought so before. I surely can't tell the Emperor that I couldn't see anything."

"Well, what do you think?" asked one of the weavers.

"Oh, I've never seen more beautiful cloth! The most beautiful in the world!" said the old minister as he put on his glasses. "What patterns and colors! Yes, I'll tell the Emperor that I'm very pleased."

"Well, we're glad you like it," said the weavers. Then they told the minister the names of the colors and the patterns, so that the minister could tell the Emperor. And he did.

The pretenders also asked for more money, more silk, and more gold. They needed the gold for weaving, they said. When they received these things they put them away in a safe place. Not one piece of material ever touched a loom. Still, they continued to weave on the empty looms.

A short time later the Emperor sent another able minister to see if his clothes were almost ready. This minister also looked and looked at the looms. But of course, there was nothing to see. "A pretty piece of cloth, don't you think?" asked the weavers. They pretended to show the patterns and colors to him.

"Surely I'm not foolish," thought the man. "Am I unfit for my job? Hmmm, is this a game? Well, I mustn't let anyone know I didn't see the cloth." And so he agreed with the weavers that the cloth was

The Emperor's New Clothes

indeed beautiful. And that is what he told the Emperor.

Soon, everyone in town was talking about the wonderful cloth.

At this time the Emperor also wanted to see the cloth. So into the weaver's room he went. But he did not go alone. He went with many of the great people in his kingdom, including the two ministers.

"Just look at this lovely cloth, your Majesty," said the two ministers. Neither of them could see anything. However, both of them believed that all the others could see the cloth.

"What's wrong here?" thought the Emperor, for he could see nothing. "What happened to my sight? This is very bad. Could it be that I am foolish? Am I unfit to be Emperor? Oh, what shall I do?"

"Oh, it is very fine indeed," said the

Emperor to the others. "I shall be quite happy to wear these clothes," he said smiling. The whole group of great men looked and looked; but they saw nothing either. "Yes, your Majesty, it is just fine," they all said to the Emperor. "The Grand Procession is coming soon," they also told him. "It would be a fine chance for you to wear these clothes for the first time."

From mouth to mouth was heard, "Wonderful, beautiful, lovely." And the Emperor, thinking that everyone else could see the cloth, also seemed pleased. In fact, he gave the honor of "Weavers to the Emperor" to the two pretenders.

The evening before the Grand Procession was a busy one. The weavers stayed up all night working on the looms. People could see them pretending to make the cloth into clothes. At last they said, "There, the clothes are now ready!"

The Emperor, with his helpers, then came in. The weavers pretended to hold the clothes up in the air for all to see. "Look, your Majesty, here are the stockings, here are the pants, and here is the coat. This material is very, very light. When you wear it, it will feel as though you are not wearing anything. That is the beauty of the cloth."

"Of course!" said all the gentlemen. But they could see nothing, for there was nothing to see.

"And now, we would like to ask your Majesty to please take off his clothes," said the pretenders. "We will put on the new ones for you. In front of the large mirror, please! Thank you!"

The weavers pretended to dress the Emperor in his new clothes, piece by piece. They tied this and that, pulled here and there. The Emperor turned and looked at himself in the mirror.

"What a wonderful suit it is! How nicely it fits!" cried all the people at once. "What colors! What patterns! How lovely!"

"All right, I am quite ready for the Grand Procession," said the Emperor. He looked in the mirror one last time. "Does everything fit perfectly? Let us go on." The helpers then picked up the tail of the long coat and held their hands in the air. They didn't want others to know they could see nothing.

And so, the group marched outside to begin the procession. Everyone watching from the streets and the windows said, "My, what beautiful clothes the Emperor is wearing! How perfectly they fit!" Of course, no one wanted others to know that he could see no clothes. They might think him foolish or unfit for his position. In fact, the Emperor had never received nicer words about any of his clothes.

Suddenly, a small child in the crowd cried, "Why, he's got nothing on!"

"Listen to the true words of a child," said the father. Soon, everyone was talking with his neighbor about what the child said. "He has nothing on! There is a child who says he's wearing nothing."

Finally, the whole crowd cried, "He really has nothing on!"

At that point, the Emperor heard the crowd and he knew they were right. He felt very foolish. But at the same time he thought, "I must continue with this procession until the end." So he tried to pretend that nothing was wrong and just kept marching. While behind him, his helpers continued to hold up the long coat that wasn't there.

The Steadfast Tin Soldier

読みはじめる前に

The Steadfast Tin Soldier で使われている用語です。わからない語は巻末のワードリストで確認しましょう。

- [ ] steadfast
- [ ] light-headed
- [ ] grave
- [ ] tobacco
- [ ] though
- [ ] undone
- [ ] unkind
- [ ] waterfall
- [ ] journey
- [ ] stuck
- [ ] onward
- [ ] melt

用語解説

Jack-in-the-box びっくり箱 見た目はタバコの箱だが、開けると中からピエロが飛び出す。

Nutcracker くるみ割り人形 口の部分にくるみを入れて割ることができる。

主な登場人物

Little boy 小さな男の子 誕生日のお祝いに錫の兵隊のセットをもらう。

Tin soldier 一本足の錫の兵隊 25人の錫の兵隊人形のうち一番最後に作られた。この物語の主人公。

Dancer ボール紙のお城の戸口で片足で立っている紙で作られた踊り子の人形。

Water-rat 水生ネズミ 下水道に流された錫の兵隊に通行証を要求する。

There were once twenty-five tin soldiers. All of them were brothers because they had all been made from the same kitchen spoon. They shouldered long guns and looked straight ahead. Indeed, they looked very smart in their red and blue uniforms. "Tin soldiers!" That was the first thing they heard when the little boy took the top off their box. The boy was very happy because he had received them as a birthday present. He took them out of the box and put them on the table. Each soldier looked just like the next—except for one, which had only a single leg; he was the last one to be made, and there wasn't quite enough tin left. Yet he stood just as well on his one leg as the others did on their two; and he is the hero of this story.

There were many other toys on the table, but the first one everyone noticed was a paper castle. Through its little windows you could see into the little rooms. In front of the castle were very small trees. They stood around a piece of glass which was meant to be a lake. Beautiful white birds sat on the lake. The whole scene was like a dream; and the prettiest thing of all was a girl who stood in the open doorway. She too was cut out of paper; but her skirt was of the finest cotton. A blue ribbon crossed her shoulder and was held by a large, shiny, glass diamond. This lovely little girl held both her arms up high, for she was a dancer. In fact, one of her legs was raised so high in the air that the tin soldier could not see it at all. He thought that she too had only one leg.

"Oh she would be the perfect wife for me," he thought. "But she is so pretty. She lives in a castle, and I have only a box; and there are twenty-five of us in that! Surely there isn't room for her. Still, I can get to know her." So he lay down behind a tobacco box on the table where he could easily watch the little paper dancer. She continued to stand on one leg without falling down.

When evening came, all the other tin soldiers were put in their box, and the children went to bed. Now the toys began to play on their own. They played at visiting, going to school, having battles, and going to parties. The tin soldiers made noises in their box because they also wanted to play. But they couldn't get the top off their box. The nutcracker moved in circles, the pencil wrote on the paper; there was so much movement and talking that the yellow bird also began to sing. The only two who didn't move were the tin soldier and the little dancer. She continued to stand on the point of her foot, with her arms held out; he stood very still on his single leg—always watching her.

Then the clock struck twelve midnight. Suddenly, the top flew off the tobacco box and up came a little black jack-in-the-box. There was no tobacco in the box—it was just a toy.

"Tin soldier!" cried the jack-in-the-box. "Keep your eyes to yourself!"

But the tin soldier seemed not to hear.

"All right, just you wait till tomorrow!" said the unkind jack-in-the-box.

When morning came and the children returned, the tin soldier was placed next to the window. Then something happened—it may have been the jack-in-the-box or just the wind blowing, but suddenly the window opened up and out fell the tin soldier. He fell three floors down to the ground. It was a very bad fall! His leg pointed up, and his head pointed down. Also, his long gun was stuck in a space between the stones.

The little boy and his sister went to look for him in the street. Although they almost walked on him, they could not see him. If he had called out, "Here I am!" they would have found him easily. But the tin soldier didn't think that was the right thing to do when he was in uniform.

Now it began to rain; the drops fell fast and heavy. When it was over, a pair of boys passed by. "Look!" said one of them. "There's a tin soldier. Let's put him out to sea."

So they made a little paper boat and put the tin soldier in the middle. Then they put the boat in the water which was running down the street. Away he went, and the two boys ran beside him shouting happily. My, how fast the water ran, and how big the waves! It had been a hard rain. The paper boat moved up and down, round and round. The soldier felt light-headed. But he was as steadfast as ever, not moving at all, still looking straight ahead and holding his long gun.

Suddenly, the boat entered a dark tunnel under the street. Yes, it was as dark as the box at home. "Wherever am I going now?" the tin soldier wondered. "No, I don't like this at all. Ah! If only the young dancer were here in the boat with me. I wouldn't care if it was even darker."

Just then, from its home in the tunnel, jumped a large water-rat. "Do you have a passport?" it asked. "No entry without a passport!"

But the tin soldier never said a word; he only held his gun closer. The boat moved on quickly, with the rat running behind. Ugh! How angry the rat was, and shouted, "Stop him! Stop him! He hasn't paid his money! He hasn't shown his passport!"

There was no stopping the boat, though. The water ran stronger and stronger. The tin soldier could just see a little daylight far ahead. But at the same time he heard a loud rushing noise. A less steadfast man would have been afraid. Just think! Soon, the underground stream would drop like a great waterfall into a bigger stream.

But how could he stop! It was too late. The boat raced on, and the poor tin soldier tried to be strong. No one could say that he was afraid.

Suddenly the little boat went round three or four times, then filled with water. The tin soldier stood in water up to his neck. Deeper and deeper went the boat; softer and softer became the paper. At last the water closed over the soldier's head. He thought of the lovely little dancer whom he would never see again. In his ears rang the words of a song:

"Onward, onward, warrior brave! Fear not danger, nor the grave." Then the boat came undone and out fell the tin soldier. He was quickly eaten by a fish.

Oh, how dark it was inside the fish! Even darker than before, and much less space to move. But the tin soldier had no fear. He was as steadfast as ever, his long gun still at his shoulder. The fish began to move and turn wildly, and then became quite still. Something bright passed by quickly—then all around was welcome daylight. A voice cried out, "The tin soldier!"

The fish had been caught, taken to market, sold and carried into the kitchen where the cook had cut it open. Now she picked up the soldier, holding him with her fingers. She took him into the living room so that all the family could see. Truly, they were surprised. But the tin soldier was not at all proud. They stood him up on the table. And there—well, the world is full of wonders—he saw that he was in the same room where his journey had started. There were the very same children; there were the very same toys; there was the fine paper castle with the lovely little dancer at the door. She still stood on one leg, with the other raised high in the air. Ah, she was steadfast too. The tin soldier's heart was moved. If he had not been a soldier he might have started to cry. He looked at her, and she looked at him. But not a word was spoken.

And then a strange thing happened. One of the small boys picked up the tin soldier and threw him into the oven. He had no reason for doing this; maybe the unkind jack-in-the-box made him do it.

The tin soldier stood in a bright light. The heat was strong. But he didn't know if it was because of the fire, or his burning love. His bright colors were now gone—but if it was because of his journey, or his sadness, no one knew. He looked at the pretty little dancer, and she looked at him. He felt that he was melting away, but he still stood steadfast, holding his gun. Suddenly the door flew open, and a rush of air caught the little paper girl. She flew right into the oven, straight to the waiting tin soldier. There she quickly caught fire and disappeared.

Soon after, the soldier had melted down to a small piece of tin. The next day, when the cook cleaned the oven, she found him. He was in the form of a little tin heart. And the dancer? All they found was her glass diamond, and that was as black as night.

The Ugly Duckling

読みはじめる前に

The Ugly Duckling で使われている用語です。わからない語は巻末のワードリストで確認しましょう。

- [ ] ugly
- [ ] duckling
- [ ] wheat
- [ ] turkey
- [ ] surely
- [ ] gray
- [ ] present
- [ ] quack
- [ ] hurt
- [ ] bitten
- [ ] mean
- [ ] blood-red
- [ ] purr
- [ ] sunset
- [ ] joyful
- [ ] milkcan
- [ ] grain
- [ ] springtime
- [ ] dare
- [ ] sadness
- [ ] shy

主な登場人物

Ugly duckling みにくいアヒルの子　最後に残った一番大きなタマゴから生まれた体の大きなみにくいヒナ。

Mother duck お母さん　はじめのうちはみにくいアヒルの子をかばっていたが……。

Old woman おばあさん　みにくいアヒルの子を飼うことにする。

Sonny ソニー　おばあさんに飼われているネコ。

Chicky-short-legs 短足ニワトリ　おばあさんのお気に入りの雌鳥で、よいタマゴを産む。

Farmer 農夫　水辺で氷に捕まったみにくいアヒルの子を助ける。

It was so pretty out in the country in the summertime.

The fields were full of tall, yellow corn. The wheat was turning gold. All around the fields were great, green forests and deep blue lakes. In the trees, birds were speaking many different languages to each other. Yes, it was very nice in the country.

The sun was shining on an old country house that stood near a pond. From the walls down to the water grew high plants with wide leaves. Under these leaves a mother duck lay upon her eggs in her nest. By this time she had become a little tired and lonely. She had few visitors; the other ducks enjoyed swimming in the water more than sitting and talking with her.

Finally, one egg began to break open, then another and another. The little eggs had come alive. "Peep! Peep!" was the cry from the heads that now appeared.

The mother duck welcomed them into the world. "Quick! Quick!" she told them, "Look around." So they all ran about under the green, green leaves looking here and there. Their mother watched them happily.

"How big the world is!" said the young ducklings. True, there had been very little room inside the eggs.

"Do you think that this is the whole world?" asked their mother. "Why, the world goes beyond this garden and the next, right into the farmer's field; but I have never been there. Well, I guess all of you are out." She stood up and saw that there was one more egg to go. "Oh, the biggest egg is still lying there. How much longer do I have to wait for it? I'm sick and tired of it!" And down she sat again.

"Well, how are things with you?" asked an old duck who came to pay her a visit.

"This last egg is taking such a long time!" answered the sitting duck. "It's not ready to come out yet! But look at the others! Aren't they pretty little ducklings? They look just like their father, the playboy! He never comes to see me!"

"Let me see the egg that won't open up!" said the old duck. "Believe me, it's a turkey egg. I was fooled like that myself once. What trouble those young ones were, too! They were afraid of the water. Just wouldn't go in. I tried to talk them in at first, then I tried pushing them. But it was no use. Yes, I say it's a turkey egg. Leave it alone and go teach the other children to swim!"

"No, I should sit on it a little longer," said the mother. "I've sat so long already, a few more hours won't hurt."

"As you like!" said the old duck, and she walked ducklike back to the water.

At last the big egg began to break open. "Peep! Peep!" said the baby duck as it tried to shake itself out of the egg. He was so big and ugly. The mother looked at him.

"What an ugly duckling it is!" she cried. "He doesn't look like any of the others. Surely, it can't be a turkey! Well, we'll soon find out! Into the water he goes, even if I have to push him!"

The weather was perfect the next day; the sun was shining on the green leaves and the blue water. The mother duck and her family walked down to the lake. "Quick! Quick!" cried she, and one after another dropped into the water. The water went over their heads for a moment. But soon they were all floating and moving about in the water with their legs; even the ugly gray duckling.

"No, it's no turkey!" said the mother duck. "See how nicely it uses its legs, and how straight it sits up in the water! It's my own young one! I suppose he's not so ugly after all. Rather pretty really, if you look closely. Quick! Quick! Come with me everyone into the great big world. I will present you to the duck yard. But keep close to me and watch out for the cat!"

And so they came into the duck yard.

There was a loud noise. Two families were fighting over a fish head. Finally, the cat got it.

"Look, that is the way of the world!" said the mother duck. She too would have liked the fish head. "Use your legs," she said, "and look smart. Be nice to that old duck over there, for she is the most famous duck in the yard; her family comes from Spain; and see the red tie around her leg! That is a great honor; it means that they want to keep her, so men and animals must be kind to her. Quack! Quack! Don't turn your feet in! A well-brought-up duckling keeps his feet wide apart like father and mother! Look at me! Like so! And now stick out your neck and 'Quack!'

As they did so, all the other ducks watching in the yard began to talk loudly. "Just look! Now we have all these new ones, too! There are already too many of us here! And oh, my! Look at that ugly gray duckling! Well, we don't need his kind around here!" Just then a duck flew at the big duckling and bit him in the neck.

"Leave him alone, will you!" said the mother. "He's not hurting you."

"No, but he's so big and strange-looking!" said the duck who bit him, "so, we cannot accept him!"

"You have pretty children, mother!" said the old duck with the red tie around her leg. "They are all pretty except one, which hasn't turned out well at all! I wish you could make him over again!"

"Not possible, My Lady!" said the mother of the ducklings. "He isn't pretty, but he is well mannered and swims as well as the others. Even better, I must say! I think he will grow prettier, or perhaps smaller, in time. His problem is that he was in the egg too long!"

Then she straightened some of his feathers with her mouth. "Besides, he's a boy-duck," she said, "and so his beauty is not so important! I think he'll be strong enough to fight his way along!"

"The other ducklings are very nice," said the old duck. "Please make yourself at home; and if you find a fish head you may bring it to me."

But the poor duckling who was the last born and looked so ugly had many problems. He was bitten, pushed and talked about by the other ducks and chickens. "He's too big!" they all cried. Everyone in the yard began to say mean, unkind things to him. Then they would laugh and laugh at him. The poor duckling didn't know what to do.

The Ugly Duckling

And so the first day was a very bad one for him. After that, things became even more difficult. The duckling was pushed about and bitten by them all. His own brothers and sisters kept saying, "If only the cat would eat you, you ugly thing!" while even his own mother said, "If only you were far, far away!" And the girl who fed the animals hit him with her foot.

Then he ran away from the yard. He ran past trees and plants causing little birds to fly into the air. "They fly away because I am so ugly." said the duckling. He closed his eyes and ran on. At last he came to a field where the wild ducks lived. There he lay all night long, tired and sad.

In the morning the wild ducks saw their new neighbor. "What kind of a thing are you?" they asked. The duckling tried to say hello to them.

"You are quite ugly!" said the wild ducks; "but it doesn't matter to us as long as you do not marry into the family!"

Poor thing! He had no idea of marrying! It was enough for him just to lay in peace and quiet among the water plants.

There he lay for two whole days. Then there came two wild, rather young, boy-ducks who wanted to have a good time.

"Listen, friend!" they said; "you are so ugly that we quite like you. Won't you come play with us? Nearby, in another pond, are some really sweet and pretty young girl-ducks. As ugly as you are, they'll like you just the same!"

"Pop! Pop!" came a loud sound at that moment, and the two boy-ducks fell dead. The water turned blood-red. "Pop! Pop!" came more sounds from all around the pond. Many ducks were dying and the others were flying away. It was a hunting party. The hunters were firing their guns from behind plants and trees. Blue smoke was everywhere. The hunting dogs ran through the water, picking the ducks up in their mouths. The poor, ugly duckling was so afraid. He tried to put his head under his wing. Just then, a large dog stood right in front of the duckling. His mouth was open and his eyes were shining; his large, pointed teeth were touching the duckling—and suddenly! He turned and ran off.

"Oh, thank God!" thought the duckling. "I'm so ugly that even the dog won't bite me!"

And he laid very still among the water plants while the guns continued to fire away. Much later in the day, when all was quiet, the duckling lifted his head and looked around. Then he ran as fast as he could through fields and forests. But a strong wind was blowing against him, making him tired.

Finally, in the evening, he reached a little, old house. He was so tired and afraid. The house had an old, broken door that was half-open, so the duckling looked inside.

Here lived an old woman with her cat and her hen. The cat was called Sonny. He could raise his back and make cat sounds, "Purr! Purr!" The hen had fat little legs and was called Chicky-short-legs; She made hen sounds, "Cluck! Cluck!" She laid good eggs and the old woman loved her like a child.

The next morning they saw the ugly duckling sleeping outside the door. The cat purred and the hen clucked.

"I don't believe my eyes!" said the old woman looking at the duckling. But her eyes were not very good, so she thought the duckling was a fat duck which was lost. "Now maybe I can have duck eggs too. We must wait and see."

So for three weeks the duckling was taken into the household; but he did not lay a single egg. The cat was the master in that house and the hen was the mistress. They always said: "We are the world!" because they thought that they were half the world. And the better half too! The duckling did not agree with them but the hen would not listen.

"Can you lay eggs?" she asked.

"No."

"Then be quiet!"

And the cat said. "Can you raise your back and purr?"

"No!"

"Then your opinions are not equal to

ours." So the duckling sat unhappily in the corner. Then he thought of the fresh air and sunshine. Suddenly, he had such a strong desire to float upon the water that he told the hen of his feelings.

"What's wrong with you?" asked the hen. "You're out of your mind because you have nothing to do. Lay eggs or purr, and these strange ideas will go away!"

"But it's so nice to float upon the water!" said the duckling; "so nice to go under the water and down to the bottom!"

"Oh, you must be mad!" said the hen. "Ask the cat; he's the wisest person I know. If he likes floating on the water, I'll say no more. Ask the old woman; no one in the world is wiser than she. Do you think that she likes to float on or under the water?"

"You don't understand me!" said the duckling.

"If we don't understand you, I don't know who will! You will never be wiser than the three of us! Don't make a fool of yourself, child! You should thank heaven that we are so nice to you. Didn't we let you into a warm room with food to eat? You are an ugly sort of bird and being with you is not pleasant. Believe me. I'm telling you this as your friend, because it's true! You should learn to lay eggs or purr."

"I think I will go out into the wide world," said the duckling.

"Go right ahead!" said the hen.

So the duckling went. He floated on the water happily, but the other animals didn't talk to him because he was so ugly.

And now it was fall. The leaves of the forest grew yellow and brown, and the wind blew them all around. There was a cold look high in the sky. The clouds were heavy with cold rain and snow. On a fence stood a blackbird who cried "Ow! Ow!" because it was getting so cold. Oh, the poor duckling knew it wouldn't be easy.

One evening, during a beautiful sunset, a large group of lovely birds appeared from the nearby woods. The duckling had never seen anything so beautiful. They were bright white with long, pretty necks; they were swans. After making a strange cry, they spread their wings and flew up, up and up; away from the cold fields to warmer lands and lakes. They flew so high that the duckling could hardly see them. He turned around in the water and stuck out his neck to watch them. Oh! He could not forget those beautiful and happy birds. His heart was beating loudly, his eyes were wide. He did not know the name of the birds, or where they were flying. But he loved them. How joyful it would have been if they had asked him to go along! He knew he could never hope to be like them, though.

And the winter grew colder and colder. The duckling had to keep swimming to stop the water from becoming ice. But every night more water turned to ice. Finally the poor duckling was too tired to swim anymore. He lay quite still until he became stuck in the ice.

Early the next morning a farmer passed that way. He saw the duckling, went out to it, and broke the ice with his wooden shoe. He brought the bird home to his wife, and the duckling was saved.

The children wanted to play with him, but the duckling was afraid. He flew around the room and right into the milk-can. Then he flew into the butter dish and the grain. Soon, there was milk and butter and grain everywhere. The woman shouted and tried to hit the duckling with a pot; the children, laughing and falling, tried to catch it. The door was open though, and out it flew into the freshly fallen snow. He hurried into some plants and lay there so sadly.

The poor duckling had such an unhappy and difficult winter that year. Too sad to talk about, really. He was lying in a small pond among plants when the sun began to shine warmly; the other birds began to sing because it was springtime again.

One day the duckling spread its wings; they were stronger than before, and he began to fly easily. Before he knew where he was going he had arrived in a beautiful, large garden. The tree leaves were a fresh green and the bright flowers smelled lovely. In the middle of this beautiful place was a pond. Suddenly, right in front of him, there appeared three beautiful white swans. They made a rushing sound with their wings and floated on the water. The duckling remembered seeing these lovely birds and felt a strange sadness.

"I will fly towards these fine birds! They will bite me because I am so ugly and dare to come near them; but I don't care anymore. It is better they kill me than to continue living as I have. No, I couldn't stand another winter!"

So he flew out into the pond, and swam towards the swans. When they saw the duckling they rushed towards him quickly. "Kill me and end my sadness!" cried the poor duck. He lowered his head and waited for death. But what did he see in the clear water? Himself? Was it possible? He was no longer a strange, large, dark-gray and very ugly bird; he too was a swan!

It doesn't matter at all about being born in a duck-yard if one comes from a swan's egg. The large swans now swam around and around him; they touched him with their mouths and were very friendly.

Some little children came running into the garden; they threw corn and bread on the water, and the smallest of them said: "There's a new one!" The other children also shouted, "Yes! A new one has come!" They jumped up and down and ran to get their mother and father. More bread and cakes were thrown into the water, and they all said: "The new one is the prettiest! It is so young and lovely!" And the old swans lowered their heads before him.

He felt so shy that he stuck his head under his wings and didn't know what to do. He was almost too happy, but not proud; for a good heart is never proud. He thought of how he had been so completely disliked; and now all said he was the loveliest of lovely birds. And the flowers turned towards him and the sun shone nice and warm. Then the swan spread out his feathers, raised his fine neck, and cried from the bottom of his heart: "I never dreamed of such happiness when I was an ugly duckling!"

Word List

- LEVEL 1, 2は本文で使われている全ての語を掲載しています。
  LEVEL 3以上は、中学校レベルの語を含みません。ただし、本文で特殊な意味で使われている場合、その意味のみを掲載しています。
- 語形が規則変化する語の見出しは原形で示しています。不規則変化語は本文中で使われている形になっています。
- 一般的な意味を紹介していますので、一部の語で本文で実際に使われている品詞や意味と合っていないことがあります。
- 品詞は以下のように示しています。

名名詞	代代名詞	形形容詞	副副詞	動動詞	助助動詞
前前置詞	接接続詞	間間投詞	冠冠詞	略略語	俗俗語
熟熟語	頭接頭語	尾接尾語	記記号	関関係代名詞	

A

- **a** 冠 ①1つの、1人の、ある ②〜につき
- **a.m.** 《A.M.とも》午前
- **able** 形 ①《be-to〜》(人が)〜することができる ②能力のある
- **aboard** 副 船[列車・飛行機・バス]に乗って go aboard 乗船する 前 〜に乗って
- **about** 副 ①およそ、約 ②まわりに、あたりを 前 ①〜について ②〜のまわりに[の]
- **above** 前 ①〜の上に ②〜より上で、〜以上で ③〜を超えて above all 何よりも 副 ①上に ②以上に
- **accept** 動 ①受け入れる ②同意する、認める
- **across** 前 〜を渡って、〜の向こう側に、(身体の一部に)かけて
- **act** 名 行為、行い
- **add** 動 加える、足す
- **advance** 名 進歩、前進
- **afraid** 形 ①心配して ②恐れて、こわがって be afraid of 〜を恐れる、〜を怖がる
- **after** 前 ①〜の後に[で]、〜の次に ②《前後に名詞がきて》次々に〜、何度も〜《反復・継続を表す》after all やはり、結局 after that その後 one after another 次々に、1つ[人]ずつ 副 後に[で] 接 (〜した)後に[で]
- **after-life** 名 残された人生
- **afterwards** 副 その後、のちに
- **again** 副 再び、もう一度
- **against** 前 ①〜に対して、〜に反対して、(規則など)に違反して ②〜にもたれて
- **aged** 形 ①年を取った ②《the -d》年寄りたち、老人
- **ago** 副 〜前に
- **agree** 動 ①同意する ②意見が一致する agree with (人)に同意する
- **ah** 間 《驚き・悲しみ・賞賛などを表して》ああ、やっぱり
- **ahead** 副 ①前方へ[に] ②前もって ③進歩して、有利に
- **air** 名 ①《the-》空中、空間 ②空気、《the-》大気 ③雰囲気、様子 a rush of air 一陣の風 up in the air 空中に
- **alas** 間 ああ《悲嘆・後悔・恐れなどを表す声》
- **alive** 形 ①生きている ②活気のある、生き生きとした
- **all** 形 すべての、〜中 代 全部、すべて(のもの[人]) 名 全体 副 まったく、

106

WORD LIST

すっかり **above all** 何よりも **after all** やはり, 結局 **all day long** 一日中, 終日 **all night long** 一晩中 **all on board** (船に) 乗っている全員 **all right** 大丈夫で, よろしい, 申し分ない, わかった, 承知した **most of all** とりわけ, 中でも **not at all** 少しも～でない **not ～ at all** 少しも[全然]～ない **stay up all night** 徹夜する

□ **allow** 動 ①許す, 《– … to ～》…が～するのを可能にする, …に～させておく ②与える

□ **almost** 副 ほとんど, もう少しで(～するところ)

□ **alone** 形 ただひとりの 副 ひとりで, ～だけで **leave ～ alone** ～をそっとしておく

□ **along** 前 ～に沿って 副 ～に沿って, 前へ, 進んで

□ **already** 副 すでに, もう

□ **also** 副 ～も(また), ～も同様に 接 その上, さらに

□ **although** 接 ～だけれども, ～にもかかわらず, たとえ～でも

□ **always** 副 いつも, 常に **as always** いつものように

□ **am** 動 ～である, (～に)いる[ある] 《主語がIのときのbeの現在形》

□ **among** 前 (3つ以上のもの)の間で[に], ～の中で[に]

□ **an** 冠 ①1つの, 1人の, ある ②～につき

□ **and** 接 ①そして, ～と… ②《同じ語を結んで》ますます ③《結果を表して》それで, だから **and so** そこで, それだから, それで **and yet** それなのに, それにもかかわらず

□ **angry** 形 怒って, 腹を立てて

□ **animal** 名 動物

□ **another** 形 ①もう1つ[1人]の ②別の 代 ①もう1つ[1人] ②別のもの **one after another** 次々に, 1つ[人]ずつ

□ **answer** 動 ①答える, 応じる ②《– for ～》～の責任を負う

□ **any** 形 ①《疑問文で》何か, いくつかの ②《否定文で》何も, 少しも(～ない) ③《肯定文で》どの～も 代 ①《疑問文で》(～のうち)何か, どれか, 誰か ②《否定文で》少しも, 何も[誰も]～ない ③《肯定文で》どれも, 誰でも

□ **anymore** 副 《通例否定文, 疑問文で》今はもう, これ以上, これから

□ **anyone** 代 ①《疑問文・条件節で》誰か ②《否定文で》誰も (～ない) ③《肯定文で》誰でも

□ **anything** 代 ①《疑問文で》何か, どれでも ②《否定文で》何も, どれも (～ない) ③《肯定文で》何でも, どれでも **anything else** ほかの何か 副 いくらか

□ **anytime** 副 いつでも

□ **anywhere** 副 どこかへ[に], どこにも, どこへも, どこにでも

□ **apart** 副 ①ばらばらに, 離れて ②別にして, それだけで **come apart** バラバラになる

□ **appear** 動 ①現れる, 見えてくる ②(～のように)見える, ～らしい

□ **appearance** 名 ①現れること, 出現 ②外見, 印象

□ **are** 動 ～である, (～に)いる[ある] 《主語がyou, we, they または複数名詞のときのbeの現在形》

□ **arm** 名 腕 **arm in arm** 腕を組んで

□ **army** 名 軍隊

□ **around** 副 まわりに, あちこちに 前 ～のまわりに, ～のあちこちに

□ **arrive** 動 到着する, 到達する **arrive at** ～に着く **arrive in** ～に着く

□ **art** 名 芸術, 美術

□ **as** 接 ①《as ～ as …の形で》…と同じくらい～ ②～のとおりに, ～のように ③～しながら, ～しているときに ④～するにつれて, ～にしたがって ⑤～なので ⑥～だけれども ⑦～する限りでは 前 ①～として(の) ②～の時 副 同じくらい 代 ①～のような ②～だが **as always** いつものよ

うに **as if** あたかも~のように, まるで~みたいに **as long as** ~する以上は, ~である限りは **as though** あたかも~のように, まるで~みたいに **as well** なお, その上, 同様に **as well as** ~と同様に **as ever** 相変わらず, これまでのように **as ~ as one can** できる限り~ **just as** (ちょうど)であろうとおり

- **ashore** 副 岸に, 陸上に
- **ask** 動 ①尋ねる, 聞く ②頼む, 求める **ask ~ if** ~かどうか尋ねる
- **asleep** 形 眠って(いる状態の) 副 眠って
- **at** 前 ①《場所・時》~に[で] ②《目標・方向》~に[を], ~に向かって ③《原因・理由》~を見て[聞いて・知って] ④~に従事して, ~の状態で
- **away** 副 離れて, 遠くに, 去って, わきに

B

- **baby** 形 ①赤ん坊の ②小さな
- **back** 名 背中 副 ①戻って ②後ろへ[に] **back away** 後ずさりする **come back** 戻る **come back to ~** へ帰ってくる, ~に戻る **turn back** 元に戻る
- **bad** 形 ①悪い, へたな, まずい ②気の毒な ③(程度が)ひどい, 激しい
- **ballroom** 名 ダンスホール, 舞踏場
- **battle** 名 戦闘, 戦い
- **bay** 名 湾, 入り江
- **be** 動 ~である, (~に)いる[ある], ~となる 助 ①《現在分詞とともに用いて》~している ②《過去分詞とともに用いて》~される, ~されている
- **beat** 動 打つ, 鼓動する
- **beautiful** 形 美しい, すばらしい
- **beautifully** 副 美しく, 立派に, 見事に
- **beauty** 名 ①美, 美しい人[物] ②《the -》美点
- **became** 動 become (なる)の過去
- **because** 接 (なぜなら)~だから, ~という理由[原因]で **because of** ~のために, ~の理由で
- **become** 動 ①(~に)なる ②(~に)似合う ③becomeの過去分詞 **become stuck** (異物が)詰まる
- **bed** 名 ①ベッド, 寝所 ②花壇 **go to bed** 床につく, 寝る
- **been** 動 be (~である)の過去分詞 助 be (~している・~される)の過去分詞
- **before** 前 ~の前に[で], ~より以前に 接 ~する前に 副 以前に
- **began** 動 begin (始まる)の過去
- **begin** 動 始まる[始める], 起こる
- **behind** 前 ①~の後ろに, ~の背後に ②~に遅れて, ~に劣って 副 ①後ろに, 背後に ②遅れて, 劣って
- **being** 名 存在, 生命, 人間
- **believe** 動 信じる, 信じている, (~と)思う, 考える
- **bell** 名 ベル, 鈴, 鐘
- **belong** 動《- to ~》~に属する, ~のものである
- **below** 前 ①~より下に ②~以下の, ~より劣る 副 下に[へ]
- **beneath** 前 ~の下に[の], ~より低い
- **beside** 前 ①~のそばに, ~と並んで ②~と比べると ③~とはずれて
- **besides** 前 その上, さらに
- **best** 形 最もよい, 最大[多]の
- **better** 形 ①よりよい ②(人が)回復して 副 ①よりよく, より上手に ②むしろ **even better** さらに素晴らしいことに **know better (than)** (~より)もっと分別がある
- **between** 前 (2つのもの)の間に[で・の]
- **beyond** 前 ~を越えて, ~の向こうに

Word List

- **big** 形 大きい
- **bird** 名 鳥
- **birthday** 名 誕生日
- **bit** 動 bite(かむ)の過去, 過去分詞
- **bite** 動 かむ, かじる
- **bitten** 動 bite(かむ)の過去分詞
- **black** 形 黒い, 有色の
- **blackbird** 名 クロウタドリ
- **bleed** 動 出血する, 血を流す[流させる]
- **blew** 動 blow(吹く)の過去
- **blood** 名 血, 血液
- **blood-red** 形 血で赤く染まった
- **blow** 動 (風が)吹く, (風が)〜を吹き飛ばす **blow up** 破裂する[させる]
- **blue** 形 ①青い ②青ざめた ③憂うつな, 陰気な 名 青(色)
- **blueflower** 名 ブルーフラワー《架空の花の名前》
- **bluish** 形 青みがかった
- **board** 名 板 **all on board** (船に)乗っている全員 **on board** (乗り物などに)乗って, 搭乗して
- **boat** 名 ボート, 小舟, 船
- **body** 名 体, 死体, 胴体
- **bone** 名 骨, 《-s》骨格
- **born** 動 **be born** 生まれる **be born into** 〜に生まれる
- **both** 形 両方の, 2つとも 代 両方, 両者, 双方 **both of them** 彼ら[それら]両方とも
- **bottom** 名 底, 下部
- **box** 名 箱, 容器
- **boy** 名 少年, 男の子
- **boy-duck** 名 オスの子ガモ
- **branch** 名 枝
- **brave** 形 勇敢な
- **bread** 名 パン
- **break** 動 壊す, 折る **break in two** 二つに切る, 両断する **break open** (金庫などを)こじ開ける
- **breast** 名 胸, 乳房
- **bridal** 形 花嫁の, 婚礼の
- **bride** 名 花嫁, 新婦
- **bride-to-be** 名 花嫁となる人
- **bridegroom** 名 花婿, 新郎
- **bright** 形 輝いている, 鮮明な
- **bring** 動 ①持ってくる, 連れてくる ②もたらす, 生じる **bring home** 家に持ってくる **bring up** 育てる, 連れて行く
- **broad** 形 幅の広い
- **broke** 動 break(壊す)の過去
- **broken** 形 破れた, 壊れた
- **brother** 名 兄弟
- **brought** 動 bring(持ってくる)の過去, 過去分詞
- **brown** 形 茶色の 名 茶色(のもの)
- **building** 名 建物, 建造物, ビルディング
- **built** 動 build(建てる)の過去, 過去分詞 **be built of** 〜で造られている
- **burn** 動 燃える, 燃やす
- **burning** 形 燃えている, 燃えるように熱い
- **business** 名 ①職業, 仕事 ②商売
- **busy** 形 忙しい **be busy with** 〜で忙しい
- **but** 接 ①でも, しかし ②〜を除いて **not 〜 but …** 〜ではなくて… 前 〜を除いて, 〜のほかは
- **butter** 名 バター
- **butter dish** バター皿《食卓でバターを載せる皿》
- **buy** 動 買う, 獲得する
- **by** 前 ①《位置》〜のそばに[で] ②《手段・方法・行為者・基準》〜によって, 〜で ③《期限》〜までには ④《通過・経由》〜を経由して, 〜を通って 副 そばに, 通り過ぎて

The Best of Andersen's Fairy Tales

C

- **cake** 名 菓子, ケーキ
- **call** 呼ぶ, 叫ぶ **call out** 叫ぶ, 呼び出す, 声を掛ける
- **came** 動 come（来る）の過去
- **can** 動 ①〜できる ②〜してもよい ③〜でありうる ④《否定文で》〜のはずがない **as 〜 as one can** できる限り〜 **can hardly** とても〜できない **Can you 〜?** してくれますか。
- **cannot** can（〜できる）の否定形（=can not）
- **care** 名 ①心配, 注意 ②世話, 介護 **take care of** 〜の世話をする, 〜の面倒を見る, 〜を管理する 動 ①《通例否定文・疑問文で》気にする, 心配する ②世話をする **care about** 〜を気に掛ける
- **careful** 形 注意深い, 慎重な
- **carry** 動 ①運ぶ, 連れていく, 持ち歩く ②伝わる, 伝える **carry away** 運び去る **carry into** 〜の中に運び入れる
- **castle** 名 城, 大邸宅
- **cat** 名 ネコ（猫）
- **catch** 動 ①つかまえる ②追いつく ③（病気に）かかる **catch fire** 火がつく, 引火する
- **caught** 動 catch（つかまえる）の過去, 過去分詞
- **cause** 動 （〜の）原因となる, 引き起こす
- **certainly** 副 ①確かに, 必ず ②《返答に用いて》もちろん, そのとおり, 承知しました
- **chance** 名 ①偶然, 運 ②好機
- **change** 動 ①変わる, 変える ②交換する
- **check** 動 照合する, 検査する **check on** 〜を調べる
- **chicken** 名 ニワトリ（鶏）
- **chicky-short-legs** 名 短足ニワトリ
- **child** 名 子ども
- **children** 名 child（子ども）の複数
- **choose** 動 選ぶ, （〜に）決める
- **church** 名 教会, 礼拝（堂）
- **circle** 名 円, 円周, 輪 **in a circle** 輪になって
- **city** 名 都市, 都会
- **clean** 形 きれいな, 清潔な 動 掃除する, よごれを落とす
- **clear** 形 ①はっきりした, 明白な ②澄んだ ③（よく）晴れた 副 ①はっきりと ②すっかり, 完全に
- **clearly** 副 ①明らかに, はっきりと ②《返答に用いて》そのとおり
- **clock** 名 掛け［置き］時計
- **close** 形 ①近い ②親しい ③狭い 副 ①接近して ②密集して 動 閉まる, 閉める
- **closely** 副 ①密接に ②念入りに, 詳しく ③ぴったりと
- **cloth** 名 布（地）
- **clothes** 名 衣服, 身につけるもの
- **clothing** 名 衣類, 衣料品
- **cloud** 名 雲, 雲状のもの
- **cloudy** 形 曇った, 雲の多い
- **cluck** 名 コッコッという鳴き声 動 （めんどりが）コッコッと鳴く
- **coat** 名 上着, コート
- **cold** 形 寒い, 冷たい
- **color** 名 色, 色彩
- **colored** 形 ①色のついた ②有色人種の, 黒人の
- **colorful** 形 カラフルな, 派手な
- **come** 動 ①来る, 行く, 現れる ②（出来事が）起こる, 生じる ③〜になる ④come の過去分詞 **come across** 〜に出くわす, 〜に遭遇する **come along** ①一緒に来る, ついて来る ②やって来る, 現れる ③うまくいく, よくなる, できあがる **come and 〜**しに行く **come apart** バラバラになる **come back** 戻る **come back to** 〜へ帰ってくる, 〜に戻る **come by** やって来る, 立ち寄る **come**

WORD LIST

down ～を下りて来る **come in** 中にはいる, やってくる, 出回る **come into** ～に入ってくる **come out** 出てくる, 出掛ける, 姿を現す, 発行される **come out from** ～から出てくる **come over** やって来る, ～の身にふりかかる **come running** 飛んでくる, かけつける **come to life** 目覚める, 復活する **come true** 実現する **come up** 近づいてくる, 階上に行く, 浮上する, 水面へ上ってくる, 発生する, 芽を出す

- **completely** 副 完全に, すっかり
- **continue** 動 続く, 続ける, (中断後)再開する, (ある方向に)移動していく
- **cook** 名 料理人, コック
- **cool** 形 涼しい, 冷えた 動 涼しくなる, 冷える
- **coolness** 名 涼しさ, 冷淡
- **corn** 名 トウモロコシ, 穀物
- **corner** 名 ①曲がり角, 角 ②すみ, はずれ
- **costly** 形 高価な, ぜいたくな, 高くつく
- **cotton** 名 ①綿, 綿花 ②綿織物, 綿糸
- **could** 助 ①can (～できる)の過去 ②《控え目な推量・可能性・願望などを表す》Could it be ～? ～かもしれない
- **countless** 形 無数の, 数え切れない
- **country** 名 国
- **course** 名 **of course** もちろん, 当然
- **court** 名 宮廷, 宮殿
- **court dance** 宮廷舞踊
- **cover** 動 覆う, 包む, 隠す
- **creature** 名 生物, 動物
- **cross** 動 横切る, 渡る
- **crowd** 名 群集, 雑踏, 多数, 聴衆
- **crown** 名 冠
- **cry** 動 泣く, 叫ぶ, 大声を出す, 嘆く

cry out 叫ぶ 名 泣き声, 叫び, かっさい

- **cut** 動 ①切る, 刈る ②短縮する, 削る ③cutの過去, 過去分詞 **be cut off** 切り取られる **cut down** 切り倒す, 打ちのめす **cut off** 切断する, 切り離す **cut out** 切り取る, 切り抜く **cut through** 切り開く

D

- **dance** 動 踊る, ダンスをする 名 ダンス, ダンスパーティー
- **dance hall** ダンスホール
- **dancer** 名 踊り子, ダンサー
- **dancing** 名 ダンス, 舞踏
- **danger** 名 危険, 障害, 脅威
- **dangerous** 形 危険な, 有害な
- **dare** 動 《- to ～》思い切って[あえて]～する
- **dark** 形 ①暗い, 闇の ②(色が)濃い, (髪が)黒い ③陰うつな
- **dark-gray** 形 濃い灰色の 名 濃い灰色
- **daughter** 名 娘
- **day** 名 ①日中, 昼間 ②日, 期日 ③《-s》時代, 生涯 **all day long** 一日中, 終日 **every day** 毎日 **one day** (過去の)ある日, (未来の)いつか
- **daylight** 名 日光, 昼の明かり
- **dead** 形 ①死んでいる, 活気のない, 枯れた ②まったくの 副 完全に, まったく **fall dead** 倒れて死ぬ
- **dear** 形 いとしい, 親愛なる, 大事な **dear to** (人)にとって大切な
- **dearly** 副 とても, 心から
- **death** 名 ①死, 死ぬこと ②《the -》終えん, 消滅
- **decide** 動 決定[決意]する, (～しようと)決める, 判決を下す
- **deck** 名 (船の)デッキ, 甲板, 階, 床
- **declare** 動 ①宣言する ②断言する

THE BEST OF ANDERSEN'S FAIRY TALES

- □ **deep** 形①深い, 深さ～の ②深遠な ③濃い 副深く
- □ **deeply** 副深く, 非常に
- □ **demand** 動要求する
- □ **desire** 名欲望, 欲求, 願望
- □ **destroy** 動破壊する, 絶滅させる, 無効にする
- □ **diamond** 名ダイヤモンド
- □ **did** 動do（～をする）の過去 助doの過去
- □ **die** 動死ぬ, 消滅する
- □ **different** 形異なった, 違った, 別の, さまざまな **be different from** ～と違う
- □ **difficult** 形困難な, むずかしい, 扱いにくい
- □ **dinner** 名①ディナー, 夕食 ②夕食[食事]会, 祝宴
- □ **dirty** 形①汚い, 汚れた ②卑劣な, 不正な
- □ **disappear** 動見えなくなる, 姿を消す, なくなる
- □ **dish** 名①大皿 ②料理
- □ **dislike** 動嫌う
- □ **dive** 動①飛び込む, もぐる ②急降下する[させる]
- □ **do** 助①《ほかの動詞とともに用いて現在形の否定文・疑問文をつくる》②《同じ動詞を繰り返す代わりに用いる》③《動詞を強調するのに用いる》 動～をする
- □ **does** 動do（～をする）の3人称単数現在 助doの3人称単数現在
- □ **dog** 名犬 **hunting dog** 猟犬
- □ **dolphin** 名イルカ
- □ **done** 動do（～をする）の過去分詞
- □ **door** 名ドア, 戸
- □ **doorway** 名戸口, 玄関, 出入り口
- □ **down** 副①下へ, 降りて, 低くなって ②倒れて 前～の下方へ, ～を下って **down there** 下の方で[に]
- □ **drank** 動drink（飲む）の過去

- □ **dream** 名夢, 幻想 動（～の）夢を見る, 夢想[想像]する **dream of** ～を夢見る
- □ **dress** 名ドレス, 衣服, 正装 動①服を着る[着せる] ②飾る
- □ **dressed** 形服を着た **have someone dressed** ～を着せてもらう, 着させる
- □ **drink** 動飲む 名飲み物
- □ **drop** 動①（ぽたぽた）落ちる, 落とす ②下がる, 下げる 名しずく, 落下
- □ **drown** 動おぼれる, 溺死する[させる]
- □ **duck** 名カモ, アヒル 動頭を下げる, 身をかわす
- □ **duck-yard** 名アヒルの庭[囲い場]
- □ **ducklike** 形アヒルのように
- □ **duckling** 名子ガモ
- □ **during** 前～の間（ずっと）
- □ **dying** 動die（死ぬ）の現在分詞

E

- □ **each** 形それぞれの, 各自の 代それぞれ, 各自 **each other** お互いに 副それぞれに
- □ **ear** 名耳, 聴覚
- □ **early** 形①（時間や時期が）早い ②初期の, 幼少の, 若い 副①早く, 早めに ②初期に, 初めのころに
- □ **earth** 名①《the－》地球 ②大地, 陸地, 土 ③この世 **in the earth** 地中に **on earth** 地球上で, この世の
- □ **earthly** 形地上の, 現世の
- □ **easily** 副①容易に, たやすく, 苦もなく ②気楽に
- □ **east** 名《the－》東, 東部, 東方
- □ **easy** 形①やさしい, 簡単な ②気楽な, くつろいだ
- □ **eat** 動食べる
- □ **eaten** 動eat（食べる）の過去分詞
- □ **effort** 名努力（の成果）

WORD LIST

- **egg** 名卵
- **eh** 間《略式》えっ(何ですか), もう一度言ってください《驚き・疑いを表したり, 相手に繰り返しを求める》
- **eight** 名8(の数字), 8人[個] 形8の, 8人[個]の
- **either** 形①(2つのうち)どちらかの ②どちらでも 代 どちらも, どちらでも 副①どちらか ②《否定文で》～もまた(…ない)
- **else** 副①そのほかに[の], 代わりに ②さもないと anything else ほかの何か
- **emperor** 名皇帝, 天皇
- **empty** 形空の, 空いている
- **end** 名①終わり, 終末, 死 ②果て, 末, 端 動 終わる, 終える
- **enjoy** 動楽しむ, 享受する enjoy doing ～するのが好きだ, ～するのを楽しむ
- **enough** 形十分な, (～するに)足る enough to do ～するのに十分な 副(～できる)だけ, 十分に, まったく
- **enter** 動入る enter into ～に入る
- **entry** 名入ること, 入り口
- **equal** 形等しい, 均等な, 平等な be equal to ～に等しい, ～するだけの能力がある not equal to かなわない, 及びもつかない 動匹敵する, 等しい
- **especially** 副特別に, とりわけ
- **even** 副①《強意》～でさえも, ～ですら, いっそう, なおさら ②平等に even better さらに素晴らしいことに even if たとえ～でも 形①平らな, 水平の ②等しい, 均一の ③落ち着いた
- **evening** 名夕方, 晩
- **evening star** 宵の明星, 金星
- **ever** 副①今までに, これまで, かつて, いつまでも ②《強意》いったい as ～ as ever 相変わらず, いつものように
- **every** 形①どの～も, すべての, あらゆる ②毎～, ～ごとの every day 毎日 every time ～するときはいつも
- **everyone** 代 誰でも, 皆
- **everything** 代 すべてのこと[もの], 何でも, 何もかも
- **everywhere** 副 どこにいても, いたるところに
- **except** 前 ～を除いて, ～のほかは except for ～を除いて, ～がなければ 接 ～ということを除いて
- **experience** 名経験, 体験
- **eye** 名目

F

- **face** 名顔, 顔つき
- **fact** 名事実, 真相 in fact つまり, 実は, 要するに
- **fail** 動①失敗する, 落第する[させる] ②《 – to ～》～し損なう, ～できない
- **fair** 形①快晴の ②色白の, 金髪の
- **fall** 動①落ちる, 倒れる ②(値段・温度が)下がる ③(ある状態に)急に陥る fall dead 倒れて死ぬ fall down 落ちる, 転ぶ fall in love with 恋におちる fall on ～に降りかかる fall out 落ちる, 飛び出す fall to the ground 転ぶ 名①落下, 墜落 ②滝 ③崩壊 ④秋
- **fallen** 形落ちた, 倒れた
- **family** 名家族, 家庭, 一門, 家柄
- **famous** 形有名な, 名高い
- **far** 副①遠くに, はるかに, 離れて ②《比較級を強めて》ずっと, はるかに far away 遠く離れて from far away 遠くから
- **farmer** 名農民, 農場経営者
- **farther** 副もっと遠く, さらに先に 形もっと向こうの, さらに進んだ
- **fast** 形①(速度が)速い ②(時計が)進んでいる ③しっかりした 副①速

く, 急いで ②(時計が)進んで ③しっかりと, ぐっすりと
- □ **fat** 形 太った
- □ **father** 名 父親
- □ **fear** 名 ①恐れ ②心配, 不安 **in fear** おどおどして, ビクビクして 動 ①恐れる ②心配する
- □ **fearful** 形 ①恐ろしい ②心配な, 気づかって
- □ **fearfully** 副 こわがって, こわごわ
- □ **feather** 名 羽,《-s》羽毛
- □ **fed** 動 feed (食物を与える)の過去, 過去分詞
- □ **feel** 動 感じる, (〜と)思う **feel like** 〜がほしい, 〜したい気がする, 〜のような感じがする **feel the touch of** 〜の接触を感じる
- □ **feeling** 名 ①感じ, 気持ち ②触感, 知覚
- □ **feet** 名 foot (足)の複数
- □ **fell** 動 fall (落ちる)の過去 **out fell** (外側へ)落ちた
- □ **felt** 動 feel (感じる)の過去, 過去分詞
- □ **fence** 名 囲み, さく
- □ **few** 形 ①ほとんどない, 少数の(〜しかない) ②《a-》少数の, 少しはある
- □ **field** 名 野原, 田畑
- □ **fiery** 形 火のように赤い
- □ **fifteen** 名 15(の数字), 15人[個] 形 15の, 15人[個]の
- □ **fifteenth** 名 第15番目(の人[物]), 15日 形 第15番目の
- □ **fifth** 名 第5番目(の人[物]), 5日 形 第5番目の
- □ **fight** 動 (〜と)戦う, 争う **fight over** 〜のことで言い争う
- □ **fill** 動 ①満ちる, 満たす ②《be -ed with 〜》〜でいっぱいである
- □ **finally** 副 最後に, ついに, 結局
- □ **find** 動 ①見つける ②(〜と)わかる, 気づく, 〜と考える ③得る **find out** 見つけ出す, 気がつく, 知る, 調べる, 解明する
- □ **fine** 形 ①元気な ②美しい, りっぱな, 申し分ない, 結構な ③晴れた ④細かい, 微妙な 副 りっぱに, 申し分なく
- □ **finger** 名 (手の)指
- □ **fire** 名 火, 炎, 火事 動 発射する **catch fire** 火がつく, 引火する
- □ **firework** 名 花火
- □ **first** 名 最初, 第一(の人・物) **at first** 最初は, 初めのうちは 形 ①第一の, 最初の ②最も重要な **for the first time** 初めて 副 第一に, 最初に
- □ **fish** 名 魚 動 釣りをする
- □ **fisherman** 名 漁師, (趣味の)釣り人
- □ **fishermen** 名 fisherman (漁師)の複数
- □ **fit** 動 合致[適合]する, 合致させる
- □ **five** 名 5(の数字), 5人[個] 形 5の, 5人[個]の
- □ **flag** 名 旗
- □ **flat** 形 平らな
- □ **flew** 動 fly (飛ぶ)の過去
- □ **float** 動 ①浮く, 浮かぶ ②漂流する
- □ **floor** 名 床, 階
- □ **flower** 名 花, 草花
- □ **flower bed** 花壇
- □ **flower-place** 名 花壇, 花置き場
- □ **fly** 動 ①飛ぶ, 飛ばす ②(飛ぶように)過ぎる, 急ぐ **fly about** 飛び回る, 飛び交う **fly around** 飛び回る **fly away** 飛び去る **fly off** 飛び去る **fly out** 飛び出す **fly to** 〜まで飛行機で行く
- □ **foam** 名 泡, 泡状の物質
- □ **folk** 名 (生活様式を共にする)人々
- □ **follow** 動 ついていく, あとをたどる
- □ **following** 形 《the -》次の, 次に続く

WORD LIST

- **food** 名 食物, えさ, 肥料
- **fool** 名 ①ばか者, おろかな人 ②道化師 **make a fool of** ~をばかにする 動 ばかにする, だます, ふざける
- **foolish** 形 おろかな, ばかばかしい
- **foot** 名 足
- **for** 前 ①《目的・原因・対象》~にとって, ~のために[の], ~に対して ②《期間》~間 ③《代理》~の代わりに ④《方向》~へ(向かって) **for a moment** 少しの間 **for now** 今のところ, ひとまず **for oneself** 独力で, 自分のために **for the first time** 初めて **for ~ years** ~年間, ~年にわたって 接 というわけなら~, なぜなら~, だから
- **force** 動 ①強制する, 力ずくで~する, 余儀なく~させる ②押しやる, 押し込む
- **forehead** 名 ひたい
- **forest** 名 森林
- **forever** 副 永遠に, 絶えず
- **forget** 動 忘れる, 置き忘れる
- **form** 名 形, 形式
- **forth** 前 前へ, 外へ
- **fortune** 名 ①富, 財産 ②幸運, 繁栄, チャンス ③運命, 運勢
- **found** 動 find (見つける)の過去, 過去分詞
- **fountain** 名 泉, 噴水, 源
- **four** 名 4(の数字), 4人[個] 形 4の, 4人[個]の
- **fourth** 名 第4番目(の人・物), 4日 形 第4番目の
- **fresh** 形 ①新鮮な, 生気のある ②さわやかな, 清純な ③新規の
- **freshly** 副 新しく, ~したてで, 新鮮に, はつらつと
- **friend** 名 友だち, 仲間
- **friendly** 形 親しみのある, 親切な, 友情のこもった
- **from** 前 ①《出身・出発点・時間・順序・原料》~から ②《原因・理由》~がもとで **from far away** 遠くからっと **from mouth to mouth** (うわさなどが)口から口へ **from ~ to …** ~から…まで
- **front** 名 正面, 前 **in front of** ~の前に, ~の正面に
- **fruit** 名 果実, 実
- **full** 形 ①満ちた, いっぱいの, 満期の ②完全な, 盛りの, 充実した **be full of** ~で一杯である 名 全部

G

- **gain** 動 得る
- **game** 名 ゲーム, 試合, 遊び, 競技
- **garden** 名 庭, 庭園
- **gave** 動 give (与える)の過去
- **gentle** 形 ①優しい, 温和な ②柔らかな
- **gentlemen** 名 gentleman (紳士)の複数
- **get** 動 ①得る, 手に入れる ②(ある状態に)なる, いたる ③わかる, 理解する ④~させる, ~を(…の状態に)する ⑤(ある場所に)達する, 着く **get into trouble** 面倒を起こす, 困った事になる, トラブルに巻き込まれる **get nothing on** 何も着ていない **get off** ~を取り除く[外す] **get there** そこに到着する, 目的を達成する, 成功する **get to** (事)を始める, ~に達する[到着する] **get to do** ~できるようになる, ~できる機会を得る **get to know** 知るようになる, 知り合う
- **giant** 形 巨大な, 偉大な
- **girl** 名 女の子, 少女
- **girl-duck** 名 メスの子ガモ
- **give** 動 ①与える, 贈る ②伝える, 述べる ③(~を)する **give A to someone for B** 人にBと引き換えにAを渡す **give away** 手放す **give up** あきらめる, やめる, 引き渡す
- **given** 動 give (与える)の過去分詞
- **glad** 形 ①うれしい, 喜ばしい ②《be - to ~》~してうれしい, 喜んで

The Best of Andersen's Fairy Tales

〜する
- □ **gladly** 副 喜んで, うれしそうに
- □ **glass** 名 ①ガラス(状のもの), コップ, グラス ②《-es》めがね
- □ **glasses** 名 メガネ
- □ **go** 動 ①行く, 出かける ②動く ③進む, 経過する, いたる ④(ある状態に)なる **be going to** 〜するつもりである **go aboard** 乗船する **go along** 〜に沿って行く, (人)について行く **go away** 立ち去る **go down** 下に降りる **go home** 帰宅する **go in** 中に入る, 開始する **go on** 続く, 続ける, 進み続ける, 起こる, 発生する **go out** 外出する, 外へ出る **go over** 〜を越えて行く, 〜へ渡る **go round** 〜の周りを進む, 歩き回る, 回って行く **go to bed** 床につく, 寝る **go up** ①〜に上がる, 登る ②〜に近づく, 出かける **go up to** 〜まで行く, 近づく **go with** 〜と一緒に行く, 〜と調和する, 〜にとても似合う
- □ **god** 名 神 **Thank God.** ありがたい
- □ **goddess** 名 女神
- □ **gold** 名 金, 金貨, 金製品, 金色 形 金の, 金製の, 金色の
- □ **gone** 動 go (行く) の過去分詞
- □ **good** 形 ①よい, 上手な, 優れた, 美しい ②(数量・程度が)かなりの, 相当な **have a good time** 楽しい時を過ごす
- □ **goodbye** 間 さようなら
- □ **got** 動 get (得る) の過去, 過去分詞
- □ **grain** 名 穀物, 穀類, (穀物の)粒
- □ **grand** 形 雄大な, 壮麗な
- □ **Grand Procession** 大行進
- □ **granddaughter** 名 孫娘, 女の孫
- □ **grandmother** 名 祖母
- □ **grave** 名 墓
- □ **gray** 形 ①灰色の ②どんよりした, 憂うつな ③白髪の
- □ **great** 形 ①大きい, 広大な, (量や程度が)たいへんな ②偉大な, 優れた ③すばらしい, おもしろい
- □ **green** 形 緑色の, 青々とした 名 緑色
- □ **grew** 動 grow (成長する) の過去
- □ **ground** 名 地面, 土, 土地 **fall to the ground** 転ぶ
- □ **group** 名 集団, 群
- □ **grow** 動 ①成長する, 育つ, 育てる ②増大する, 大きくなる, (次第に〜に)なる **grow -er and -er** 〜にますます〜する **grow to** 〜するようになる
- □ **guess** 動 ①推測する, 言い当てる ②(〜と)思う
- □ **gun** 名 銃, 大砲

H

- □ **had** 動 have (持つ) の過去, 過去分詞 助 have の過去《過去完了の文をつくる》
- □ **hair** 名 髪, 毛
- □ **half** 名 半分 形 半分の, 不完全な 副 半分, なかば, 不十分に
- □ **half-open** 形 半分開いた
- □ **hall** 名 公会堂, ホール, 大広間, 玄関
- □ **hand** 名 ①手 ②(時計の)針 ③援助の手, 助け **hand in hand** 手をとりあって 動 手渡す **hand in** 差し出す, 提出する
- □ **handsome** 形 端正な(顔立ちの), りっぱな, (男性が)ハンサムな
- □ **hang** 動 かかる, かける, つるす, ぶら下がる **hang on** 〜につかまる, しがみつく, がんばる
- □ **happen** 動 ①(出来事が)起こる, 生じる ②偶然[たまたま]〜する **happen to** たまたま〜する, 偶然〜する
- □ **happily** 副 幸福に, 楽しく, うまく, 幸いにも
- □ **happiness** 名 幸せ, 喜び
- □ **happy** 形 幸せな, うれしい, 幸運な, 満足して **be happy to do** 〜してう

WORD LIST

れしい、喜んで~する
- **hard** 形 ①堅い ②激しい、むずかしい ③熱心な、勤勉な ④無情な、耐えがたい、厳しい、きつい 副 ①一生懸命に ②激しく ③堅く
- **hardly** 副 ①ほとんど~でない、わずかに ②厳しく、かろうじて **can hardly** とても~できない
- **has** 動 have (持つ) の3人称単数現在 助 haveの3人称単数現在《現在完了の文をつくる》
- **hat** 名 (縁のある) 帽子
- **have** 動 ①持つ、持っている、抱く ②(~が) ある、いる ③食べる、飲む ④経験する、(病気に) かかる ⑤催す、開く ⑥(人に) ~させる **have to** ~しなければならない **don't have to** ~する必要はない **have a good time** 楽しい時を過ごす **have no idea** わからない **have someone dressed** ~を着せてもらう、着させる **have something made** ~を作らせる **have the nerve** 勇気がある 助《〈have + 過去分詞〉の形で現在完了の文をつくる》~した、~したことがある、ずっと~している **would have … if ~** もし~だったとしたら…しただろう
- **he** 代 彼は[が]
- **head** 名 頭 動 向かう、向ける **head for** ~に向かう、~の方に進む
- **healthy** 形 健康な、健全な、健康によい
- **hear** 動 聞く、聞こえる **hear about** ~について聞く **hear of** ~について聞く
- **heard** 動 hear (聞く) の過去、過去分詞
- **heart** 名 ①心臓、胸 ②心、感情、ハート ③中心、本質 **with all one's heart** 心から
- **heat** 名 熱、暑さ
- **heaven** 名 ①天国 ②天国のようなところ[状態]
- **heavenly** 形 ①天の、天国のような ②すばらしい
- **heavy** 形 重い、激しい、つらい
- **held** 動 hold (つかむ) の過去、過去分詞
- **hello** 間 こんにちは、やあ **say hello to** ~によろしく言う
- **help** 動 ①助ける、手伝う ②給仕する
- **helper** 名 助手、助けになるもの
- **hen** 名 雌鳥
- **her** 代 ①彼女を[に] ②彼女の
- **here** 副 ①ここに[で] ②《- is [are] ~》ここに~がある ③さあ、そら **here and there** あちこちで **here are ~** こちらは~です。 **here is ~** こちらは~です。
- **hero** 名 英雄、ヒーロー
- **hers** 代 彼女のもの
- **herself** 代 彼女自身
- **hidden** 動 hide (隠れる) の過去分詞
- **high** 形 高い 副 高く
- **highly** 副 ①大いに、非常に ②高く評価して **think highly of** ~を高く評価する、尊敬する
- **hill** 名 丘、塚
- **him** 代 彼を[に]
- **himself** 代 彼自身
- **his** 代 ①彼の ②彼のもの
- **hit** 動 ①打つ、なぐる ②ぶつける、ぶつかる ③命中する ④(天災などが) 襲う、打撃を与える ⑤hitの過去、過去分詞
- **hmmm** 間 ①《驚き》ふん！ ②えっ？
- **hold** 動 ①つかむ、持つ、抱く ②保つ、持ちこたえる ③収納できる、入れることができる ④(会などを) 開く **hold out** 差し出す、(腕を) 伸ばす **hold up** ①維持する、支える ②~を持ち上げる ③(指を) 立てる
- **holy** 形 聖なる、神聖な
- **holy temple** 聖堂
- **home** 名 家 **at home** 自宅で、在

THE BEST OF ANDERSEN'S FAIRY TALES

宅して, くつろいで **make oneself at home** くつろぐ 副家に, 自国へ **bring home** 家に持ってくる

- □ **honor** 名①名誉, 光栄, 信用 ②節操, 自尊心 **honor of** ～の名誉
- □ **hope** 動望む, (～であるようにと)思う
- □ **horse** 名馬
- □ **hot** 形暑い, 熱い
- □ **hour** 名1時間, 時間
- □ **house** 名家
- □ **household** 名家族, 世帯
- □ **how** 副①どうやって, どれくらい, どんなふうに ②なんて (～だろう) ③《関係副詞》～する方法 **How about ～?** ～はどうですか。～しませんか。
- □ **however** 接けれども, だが
- □ **human** 形人間の, 人の 名人間
- □ **human being** 人間
- □ **hundred** 名①100(の数字), 100人[個] ②《-s》何百, 多数 **hundreds of** 何百もの 形①100の, 100人[個]の ②多数の
- □ **hunter** 名狩りをする人, 狩人, ハンター
- □ **hunting** 名狩り, 狩猟, ハンティング, 捜索 形狩猟の
- □ **hunting dog** 猟犬
- □ **hunting party** 狩猟パーティー
- □ **hurry** 動急ぐ, 急がせる, あわてる
- □ **hurt** 動傷つける, 痛む, 害する

I

- □ **I** 代私は[が]
- □ **ice** 名①氷 ②氷菓子
- □ **idea** 名考え, 意見, アイデア, 計画 **have no idea** わからない
- □ **if** 接もし～ならば, たとえ～でも, ～かどうか **as if** あたかも～のように, まるで～みたいに **ask ～ if** ～かど

うか尋ねる **even if** たとえ～でも **if only** ～でありさえすれば **see if** ～かどうかを確かめる **would have … if ～** もし～だったとしたら…しただろう

- □ **immortal** 形①死ぬことのない, 不死の ②不滅の
- □ **immortal soul** 不死の魂
- □ **important** 形重要な, 大切な, 有力な
- □ **in** 前①《場所・位置・所属》～(の中)に[で・の] ②《時》～(の時)に[の・で], ～後(に), ～の間(に) ③《方法・手段》～で ④～を身につけて, ～を着て ⑤～に関して, ～について ⑥《状態》～の状態で 副中へ[に], 内へ[に]
- □ **include** 動含む, 勘定に入れる
- □ **including** 前～を含めて, 込みで
- □ **indeed** 副①実際, 本当に ②《強意》まったく 間本当に, まさか
- □ **inside** 名内部, 内側 形内部[内側]にある 副内部[内側]に 前～の内部[内側]に
- □ **instead** 副その代わりに
- □ **interested** 形興味を持った, 関心のある
- □ **into** 前①《動作・運動の方向》～の中へ[に] ②《変化》～に[へ]
- □ **is** 動 be (～である)の3人称単現在
- □ **it** 代①それは[が], それを[に] ②《天候・日時・距離・寒暖などを示す》**It is ～ for someone to …** (人)が…するのは～だ **So be it.** それならそれでいい。
- □ **its** 代それの, あれの
- □ **itself** 代それ自体, それ自身

J

- □ **jack-in-the-box** 名びっくり箱
- □ **job** 名仕事, 職, 雇用
- □ **journey** 名(遠い目的地への)旅

Word List

- **joy** 名 喜び, 楽しみ
- **joyful** 形 楽しませる, 喜びに満ちた
- **jump** 動 ①跳ぶ, 跳躍する, 飛び越える, 飛びかかる ②(~を)熱心にやり始める **jump up and down** 飛び跳ねる
- **just** 副 ①まさに, ちょうど, (~した)ばかり ②ほんの, 単に, ただ~だけ ③ちょっと **just as** (ちょうど)であろうとおり **just then** そのとたんに

K

- **keep** 動 ①とっておく, 保つ, 続ける ②(~を…に)しておく
- **kept** 動 keep (とっておく)の過去, 過去分詞
- **kill** 動 殺す, 消す, 枯らす
- **kind** 形 親切な, 優しい **be kind to** ~に親切である 名 種類
- **king** 名 王, 国王
- **kingdom** 名 王国
- **kiss** 名 キス 動 キスする
- **kitchen** 名 台所, 調理場
- **kitchen spoon** 大型スプーン
- **knew** 動 know (知っている)の過去
- **know** 動 ①知っている, 知る, (~が)わかる, 理解している ②知り合いである **get to know** 知るようになる, 知り合う **know better (than)** (~より)もっと分別がある **know nothing of** ~のことを知らない **know of** ~について知っている

L

- **lady** 名 婦人, 夫人, 淑女, 奥さん
- **laid** 動 lay (置く)の過去, 過去分詞
- **lake** 名 湖, 湖水, 池
- **land** 名 陸地, 土地
- **language** 名 言語, 言葉, 国語, ~語, 専門語
- **large** 形 ①大きい, 広い ②大勢の, 多量の
- **last** 形 ①《the -》最後の ②この前の, 先~ ③最新の **the last time** この前~したとき 副 ①最後に ②この前 名 《the -》最後(のもの), 終わり **at last** ついに, とうとう
- **late** 形 ①遅い, 後期の ②最近の 副 ①遅れて, 遅く ②最近まで, 以前
- **later** 形 もっと遅い, もっと後の 副 後で, 後ほど
- **laugh** 動 笑う **laugh at** ~を見て[聞いて]笑う 名 笑い(声)
- **lay** 動 ①置く, 横たえる, 敷く ②整える ③卵を産む ④lie (横たわる)の過去
- **lead** 動 導く **lead into** (ある場所)へ導く
- **leaf** 名 葉
- **learn** 動 学ぶ, 習う, 教わる, 知識[経験]を得る
- **leave** 動 ①出発する, 去る ②残す, 置き忘れる ③(~を…の)ままにしておく ④ゆだねる **leave ~ alone** ~をそっとしておく
- **leaves** 名 leaf (葉)の複数
- **led** 動 lead (導く)の過去, 過去分詞
- **left** 動 leave (去る, ~をあとに残す)の過去, 過去分詞
- **leg** 名 ①脚, すね ②支柱
- **lemon** 名 レモン
- **less** 形 ~より小さい[少ない] 副 ~より少なく, ~ほどでなく **much less** まして~でない
- **let** 動 (人に~)させる, (~するのを)許す, (~をある状態に)する **Let me see.** ええと。 **let out** (声を)出す, 発する **let us** どうか私たちに~させてください
- **lie** 動 ①うそをつく ②横たわる, 寝る ③(ある状態に)ある, 存在する **lie down** 横たわる, 横になる **lie nearby** すぐ近くに位置する

THE BEST OF ANDERSEN'S FAIRY TALES

- **life** 名①生命, 生物 ②一生, 生涯, 人生 ③生活, 暮らし, 世の中 **come to life** 目覚める, 復活する
- **lift** 動持ち上げる, 上がる
- **light** 名光, 明かり 形①明るい ②(色が)薄い, 淡い ③軽い, 容易な
- **light-headed** 形①軽薄な ②(酒などで)ふらふらする
- **lightly** 副①軽く, そっと ②軽率に
- **lightning** 名電光, 雷, 稲妻
- **like** 動好む, 好きである **would like to** ~したいと思う 前~に似ている, ~のような **feel like** ~がほしい, ~したい気がする, ~のような感じがする **like this** このように, こんなふうに **look like** ~のように見える, ~に似ている **sound like** ~のように聞こえる 形似ている, ~のような 接あたかも~のように 名①好きなもの ②《the [one's] –》同じようなもの[人]
- **line** 名線, 糸
- **listen** 動《– to ~》~を聞く, ~に耳を傾ける
- **lit** 動light (火をつける)の過去, 過去分詞
- **little** 形①小さい, 幼い ②少しの, 短い ③ほとんど~ない,《a –》少しはある 副全然~ない,《a –》少しはある
- **live** 動住む, 暮らす, 生きている **there lived ~.** ~が住んでいました。
- **lives** 名life (生命)の複数
- **living** 形生きている, 現在の
- **living room** リビングルーム, 居間
- **lonely** 形①孤独な, 心さびしい ②ひっそりした, 人里離れた
- **long** 形①長い, 長期の ②《長さ・距離・時間などを示す語句を伴って》~の長さ[距離・時間]の **a long way off** 遠く離れている, 遠方にある **as long as** ~する以上は, ~である限りは **long way** はるかに 副長い間, ずっと **all day long** 一日中, 終日 **all night long** 一晩中 **long to** ~することを切望する **no longer** もはや~ない[~しない]
- **look** 動①見る ②(~に)見える, (~の)顔つきをする ③注意する ④《間投詞のように》ほら, ねえ **look around** まわりを見回す **look down** 見下ろす **look for** ~を探す **look in** 中を見る, 立ち寄る **look into** ①~を検討する, ~を研究する ②~の中を見る, ~をのぞき込む **look like** ~のように見える, ~に似ている **look through** ~をのぞき込む **look to be** ~になりそうである **look up** 見上げる, 調べる
- **loom** 名織り機
- **lost** 動lose (失う)の過去, 過去分詞 形①失った, 負けた ②道に迷った, 困った
- **lot** 名たくさん, たいへん,《a – of ~ / -s of ~》たくさんの~
- **loud** 形大声の, 騒がしい 副大声に[で]
- **loudly** 副大声で, 騒がしく
- **love** 名愛, 愛情, 思いやり **fall in love with** 恋におちる 動愛する, 恋する, 大好きである
- **loveliness** 名愛らしさ, 美しさ
- **lovely** 形愛らしい, 美しい, すばらしい
- **loving** 形愛する, 愛情のこもった
- **low** 形低い, 弱い
- **lower** 動下げる, 低くする
- **lying** 動lie (横たわる)の現在分詞

M

- **machine** 名機械, 仕掛け, 機関
- **mad** 形①気の狂った ②逆上した, 理性をなくした
- **made** 動make (作る)の過去, 過去分詞 形作った, 作られた **be made from** ~から作られる **be made of**

Word List

〜でできて[作られて]いる have something made 〜を作らせる
- **magic** 名 ①魔法, 手品 ②魔力 形 魔法の, 魔力のある
- **majesty** 名《M-》陛下
- **make** 動 ①作る, 得る ②行う, (〜に)なる ③(〜を…に)する, (〜を…)させる make a fool of 〜をばかにする make into 〜に仕立てる make oneself at home くつろぐ make sure 確かめる, 確認する
- **man** 名 男性, 人, 人類
- **mankind** 名 人類, 人間
- **mannered** 形 行儀[態度]が〜の
- **many** 形 多数の, たくさんの many a いくつもの〜, 数々の〜
- **marble** 名 大理石
- **march** 動 行進する[させる]
- **market** 名 市場, マーケット
- **marry** 動 結婚する
- **marrying** 名 結婚(すること)
- **mast** 名 マスト, 帆柱
- **master** 名 主人, 雇い主
- **material** 名 材料, 原料
- **matter** 名 物, 事, 事件, 問題 not matter 問題にならない
- **may** 助 ①〜かもしれない ②〜してもよい, 〜できる
- **maybe** 副 たぶん, おそらく
- **me** 代 私を[に]
- **mean** 動 ①意味する ②(〜のつもりで)言う, 意図する ③〜するつもりである 形 卑怯な, けちな, 意地悪な
- **meant** 動 mean (意味する)の過去, 過去分詞
- **meet** 動 会う
- **melt** 動 溶ける, 溶かす melt away 溶けてなくなる
- **men** 名 man (男性)の複数
- **mermaid** 名 (女の)人魚
- **merman** 名 (男の)人魚
- **mermen** 名 merman((男の)人魚)の複数
- **middle** 名 中間, 最中 in the middle of 〜の真ん中[中ほど]に
- **midnight** 名 夜の12時, 真夜中, 暗黒
- **might** 助《mayの過去》①〜かもしれない ②〜してもよい, 〜できる
- **mile** 名 ①マイル《長さの単位. 1,609m》②《-s》かなりの距離
- **milk** 名 牛乳, ミルク
- **milkcan** 名 (運搬用)牛乳缶
- **mind** 名 心, 精神, 考え
- **minister** 名 大臣, 閣僚
- **minute** 名 ①(時間の)分 ②ちょっとの間
- **mirror** 名 鏡
- **mistress** 名 女主人, 女性の支配者
- **moment** 名 ①瞬間, ちょっとの間 ②(特定の)時, 時期 at that moment その時に, その瞬間に for a moment 少しの間
- **money** 名 金, 通貨
- **moon** 名 月, 月光
- **moonlight** 名 月明かり, 月光
- **moonshine** 名 月光, 月明かり
- **more** 形 ①もっと多くの ②それ以上の, 余分の 副 もっと, さらに多く, いっそう more and more ますます more than 〜以上 no more もうない once more もう一度
- **morning** 名 朝, 午前
- **most** 形 ①最も多い ②たいていの, 大部分の 代 ①大部分, ほとんど ②最多数, 最大限 at the most せいぜい, 多くて most of all とりわけ, 中でも 副 最も(多く)
- **mother** 名 母, 母親
- **mountain** 名 山
- **mouth** 名 口 from mouth to mouth (うわさなどが)口から口へ
- **move** 動 動く, 動かす, 移動する be moved 感激する, 感銘す

121

る move about 動き回る move around あちこち移動する move in 引っ越す move on 先に進む

- **movement** 名 ①動き, 運動 ②変動
- **much** 形《量・程度が》多くの, 多量の 副 ①とても, たいへん ②《比較級・最上級を修飾して》ずっと, はるかに much less まして~でない too much 過度の
- **music** 名 音楽, 楽曲
- **musical** 形 音楽の
- **must** 助 ①~しなければならない ②~に違いない
- **my** 代 私の 間 おやまあ Oh my! おやまあ, まあ!
- **myself** 代 私自身

N

- **name** 名 ①名前 ②名声 ③《-s》悪口 by name 名前で, 名前だけは
- **near** 前 ~の近くに, ~のそばに 副 近くに, 親密で
- **nearby** 形 近くの, 間近の 副 近くで, 間近で
- **nearly** 副 ①近くに, 親しく ②ほとんど, あやうく
- **neck** 名 首
- **need** 動 (~を)必要とする, 必要である need to do ~する必要がある
- **neighbor** 名 隣人
- **neighboring** 形 隣の, 近所の
- **neither** 代 (2者のうち)どちらも~でない 副《否定文に続いて》も…しない neither ~ nor … ~も…もない
- **nerve** 名 ①神経 ②気力, 精力 have the nerve 勇気がある
- **nest** 名 ①巣 ②居心地よい場所, 休憩所, 隠れ家
- **never** 副 決して[少しも]~ない, 一度も[二度と]~ない

- **new** 形 ①新しい, 新規の ②新鮮な, できたての
- **next** 形 ①次の, 翌~ ②隣の next to ~のとなりに, ~の次に 副 ①次に ②隣に 代 次の人[もの]
- **nice** 形 すてきな, よい, きれいな, 親切な
- **nicely** 副 ①うまく, よく ②上手に, 親切に, 几帳面に
- **night** 名 夜, 晩 all night long 一晩中 stay up all night 徹夜する
- **no** 副 ①いいえ, いや ②少しも~ない no longer もはや~でない[~しない] no more もう~ない no use 役に立たない, 用をなさない 形 ~がない, 少しも~ない, ~どころでない, ~禁止
- **no one** 誰も[一人も]~ない
- **nobody** 代 誰も[1人も]~ない
- **noise** 名 騒音, 騒ぎ, 物音
- **none** 代 (~の)何も[誰も・少しも]…ない
- **nor** 接 ~もまたない neither ~ nor … ~も…もない
- **nose** 名 鼻, 嗅覚, におい
- **not** 副 ~でない, ~しない not at all 少しも~でない not equal to かなわない, 及びもつかない not matter 問題にならない not quite まったく~だというわけではない not yet まだ~してない not ~ at all 少しも[全然]~ない not ~ but … ~ではなくて…
- **nothing** 代 何も~ない[しない] get nothing on 何も着ていない know nothing of ~のことを知らない
- **notice** 動 ①気づく, 認める ②通告する
- **now** 副 ①今(では), 現在 ②今すぐに ③では, さて now that 今や~だから, ~からには 名 今, 現在 by now 今のところ, 今ごろまでには for now 今のところ, ひとまず
- **number** 名 ①数, 数字, 番号 ②~

122

WORD LIST

- 号, ~番 ③《-s》多数 **a number of** いくつかの~, 多くの~
- **nutcracker** 名 クルミ割り器

O

- **ocean** 名 海, 大洋
- **of** 前 ①《所有・所属・部分》~の, ~に属する ②《性質・特徴・材料》~の, ~製の ③《部分》~のうち ④《分離・除去》~から
- **off** 副 ①離れて ②はずれて ③止まって ④休んで **a long way off** 遠く離れている, 遠方にある 形 ①離れて ②季節はずれの ③休みの 前 ~を離れて, ~をはずれて, (値段が) ~引きの
- **office** 名 ①会社, 事務所, 職場, 役所, 局 ②官職, 地位, 役
- **often** 副 しばしば, たびたび
- **oh** 間 ああ, おや, まあ **Oh my!** おやまあ, まあ！
- **old** 形 ①年取った, 老いた ②~歳の ③古い, 昔の
- **on** 前 ①《場所・接触》~(の上) に ②《日・時》~に, ~と同時に, ~のすぐ後で ③《関係・従事》~に関して, ~について, ~して 副 ①身につけて, 上に ②前へ, 続けて
- **once** 副 ①一度, 1回 ②かつて **once more** もう一度 名 一度, 1回 **at once** すぐに, 同時に
- **one** 名 1(の数字), 1人[個] 形 ①1の, 1人[個]の ②ある~ ③《the-》唯一の **one day** (過去の) ある日, (未来の) いつか 代 ①(一般の) 人, ある物 ②一方, 片方 ③~なもの **one after another** 次々に, 1つ[人] ずつ **one of** ~の1つ[人] **one upon the other** 次から次へと重ねる
- **only** 形 唯一の 副 ①単に, ~にすぎない, ただ~だけ ②やっと **if only** ~でありさえすれば 接 ただし, だがしかし
- **onward** 副 前方へ, 進んで
- **open** 形 ①開いた, 広々とした ②公開された **break open** (金庫などを) こじ開ける 動 ①開く, 始まる ②広がる, 広げる ③打ち明ける **open up** 広がる, 広げる, 開く, 開ける
- **open sea** 外海
- **opinion** 名 意見, 見識, 世論, 評判
- **or** 接 ①~か…, または ②さもないと ③すなわち, 言い換えると
- **orange** 名 オレンジ 形 オレンジ色の
- **other** 形 ①ほかの, 異なった ②(2つのうち) もう一方の, (3つ以上のうち) 残りの 代 ①ほかの人[物] ②《the-》残りの1つ 太字>one upon the other 次から次へと重ねる
- **our** 代 私たちの
- **ours** 代 私たちのもの
- **out** 副 ①外へ[に], 不在で, 離れて ②世に出て ③消えて ④すっかり **out of** ①~から外へ, ~から抜け出して ②~から作り出して 形 ①外の, 遠く離れた ②公表された 前 ~から外へ[に]
- **outside** 副 外へ, 外側に 前 ~の外に[で・の・よ], ~の範囲を越えて
- **oven** 名 かまど, 天火, オーブン
- **over** 前 ①~の上の[に], ~を一面に覆って ②~を越えて, ~以上に, ~よりも多って ③~の向こう側の[に] ④~の間ずっと 副 上に, 一面に, ずっと 形 ①上部の, 上位の, 過多の ②終わって, すんで **be over** 終わる
- **overhead** 形 頭上に, 真上に
- **ow** 間 オウ《鳴き声》
- **own** 形 自身の **on one's own** 自力で
- **oyster** 名 カキ (牡蠣)

P

- **paid** 動 pay (払う) の過去, 過去分詞
- **pain** 名 痛み, 苦悩

- **painful** 形 痛い, 苦しい, 痛ましい
- **painting** 名 絵画, 油絵
- **pair** 名 (2つから成る)一対, 一組, ペア
- **palace** 名 宮殿, 大邸宅
- **pants** 名 ズボン, スラックス
- **paper** 名 紙
- **parent** 名《-s》両親
- **part** 名 部分, 割合
- **party** 名 ①パーティー, 会, 集まり ②派, 一行, 隊, 一味 **throw a party** パーティーを開く
- **pass** 動 過ぎる, 通る **pass by** ～のそばを通る[通り過ぎる] **pass through** ～を通る, 通行する
- **passport** 名 (通行)許可証
- **past** 前《時間・場所》～を過ぎて, ～を越して
- **pattern** 名 柄, 型, 模様
- **pay** 動 支払う, 払う, 報いる
- **payment** 名 支払い, 払い込み
- **peace** 名 ①平和, 和解 ②平穏, 静けさ **in peace** 平和のうちに, 安心して
- **pearl** 名 真珠
- **peep** 名 ピーピーという声
- **pencil** 名 鉛筆
- **people** 名 ①(一般に)人々 ②民衆, 世界の人々, 国民, 民族 ③人間
- **perfect** 形 ①完璧な, 完全な ②純然たる
- **perfectly** 副 完全に, 申し分なく
- **perhaps** 副 たぶん, ことによると
- **person** 名 ①人 ②人格, 人柄
- **pick** 動 ①(花・果実などを)摘む, もぐ ②選ぶ, 精選する ③つつく, ついて穴をあける, ほじくり出す ④(～を)摘み取る **pick up** 拾い上げる, 車で迎えに行く, 習得する, 再開する, 回復する
- **piece** 名 ①一片, 部分 ②1個, 1本 ③作品 **piece by piece** 一つ一つ
- **pink** 形 ピンク色の 名 ピンク色
- **place** 名 ①場所, 建物 ②余地, 空間 動 ①置く, 配置する ②任命する, 任じる
- **plant** 名 植物, 草木 動 植えつける
- **play** 動 ①遊ぶ, 競技する ②(楽器を)演奏する, (役を)演じる **play with** ～で遊ぶ, ～と一緒に遊ぶ
- **playboy** 名 プレイボーイ
- **pleasant** 形 ①(物事が)楽しい, 心地よい ②快活な, 愛想のよい
- **please** 動 喜ばす, 満足させる 間 どうぞ, お願いします
- **pleased** 形 喜んだ, 気に入った
- **pleasure** 名 喜び, 楽しみ, 満足, 娯楽
- **point** 名 ①先, 先端 ②点 ③地点, 時点, 箇所 ④《the -》要点 **on the point of** 今にも～しそうで 動 ①(～を)指す, 向ける ②とがらせる
- **pointed** 形 先のとがった, 鋭い
- **polypi** 名 polypus(ポリプ《イソギンチャク, ヒドラなど》)の複数
- **pond** 名 池
- **poor** 形 ①貧しい, 乏しい, 粗末な, 貧弱な ②劣った, へたな ③不幸な, 哀れな, 気の毒な
- **pop** 名 パン[ポン]という音, 発砲
- **position** 名 ①位置, 場所, 姿勢 ②地位, 身分, 職 ③立場, 状況
- **possible** 形 ①可能な ②ありうる, 起こりうる
- **pot** 名 壺, (深い)なべ
- **power** 名 力, 能力, 才能, 勢力, 権力
- **preparation** 名 準備, したく
- **prepare** 動 準備[用意]をする
- **present** 名 贈り物, プレゼント 動 紹介する
- **presently** 副 ①やがて, じき ②今, 目下
- **pretend** 動 ふりをする, 装う

WORD LIST

- □ **pretender** 名 ~のふりをする人，詐称する人
- □ **pretty** 形 ①かわいい，きれいな ②相当の 副 かなり，相当，非常に
- □ **pretty-smelling** 形 美しい香りのする
- □ **priced** 形 価格のつけられた
- □ **priest** 名 聖職者，牧師，僧侶
- □ **prince** 名 王子，プリンス
- □ **princess** 名 王女
- □ **problem** 名 問題，難問
- □ **procession** 名 行進，行列
- □ **promise** 動 ①約束する ②見込みがある
- □ **proud** 形 ①自慢の，誇った，自尊心のある ②高慢な，尊大な **be proud of** ~を自慢に思う
- □ **pull** 動 ①引く，引っ張る ②引きつける
- □ **purr** 動 (猫などが)のどを鳴らす 名 のどをゴロゴロ鳴らす音［こと］
- □ **push** 動 ①押す，押し進む，押し進める ②進む，突き出る
- □ **put** 動 ①置く，のせる ②入れる，つける ③(ある状態に)する ④put の過去，過去分詞 **put away** 片づける，取っておく **put in** ~の中に入れる **put on** ①~を身につける，着る ②~を…の上に置く **put out** ①外に出す，(手など)を(差し)出す ②(明かり・火を)消す

Q

- □ **quack** 名 アヒルの鳴き声，ガーガー，クワックワッ 動 (アヒルなどが)ガーガー鳴く
- □ **question** 名 質問，疑問，問題 動 ①質問する ②調査する ③疑う
- □ **quick** 形 (動作が)速い，すばやい 副 速く，急いで，すぐに
- □ **quickly** 副 敏速に，急いで
- □ **quiet** 形 ①静かな，穏やかな，じっとした ②おとなしい，無口な，目立たない
- □ **quietly** 副 ①静かに ②平穏に，控えめに
- □ **quite** 副 ①まったく，すっかり，完全に ②かなり，ずいぶん ③ほとんど **not quite** まったく~だというわけではない

R

- □ **race** 動 疾走する
- □ **rain** 名 雨，降雨 動 雨が降る
- □ **raise** 動 ①上げる，高める ②起こす
- □ **ran** 動 run (走る)の過去
- □ **rang** 動 ring (鳴る)の過去
- □ **rat** 名 ネズミ(鼠)
- □ **rather** 副 ①むしろ，かえって ②かなり，いくぶん，やや ③それどころか逆に **rather than** ~よりむしろ **would rather** ~する方がよい
- □ **reach** 動 ①着く，到着する，届く ②手を伸ばして取る **reach down** 手を下に伸ばす
- □ **ready** 形 用意［準備］ができた，まさに~しようとする，今にも~せんばかりの **be ready for** 準備が整って，~に期待する **be ready to** すぐに［いつでも］~できる，~する構えで
- □ **realize** 動 理解する，実現する
- □ **really** 副 本当に，実際に，確かに
- □ **reason** 名 ①理由 ②理性，道理 **reason for** ~の理由
- □ **receive** 動 ①受け取る，受領する ②迎える，迎え入れる
- □ **red** 形 赤い 名 赤，赤色
- □ **regain** 動 取り戻す，(~に)戻る
- □ **remember** 動 思い出す，覚えている，忘れないでいる
- □ **rest** 動 ①休む，眠る ②休止する，静止する
- □ **return** 動 帰る，戻る，返す 名 ①帰

還, 返却 ②返答, 報告(書), 申告 **in return for** ~に対する見返りとして, ~の交換条件として
- **ribbon** 名 リボン
- **ride** 動 乗る, 乗って行く, 馬に乗る
- **right** 形 ①正しい ②適切な ③健全な ④右(側)の **all right** 大丈夫で, よろしい, 申し分ない, わかった, 承知した 副 ①まっすぐに, すぐに ②右(側)に ③ちょうど, 正確に **walk right up** まっすぐ歩いて上る
- **ring** 動 (ベルなどが)鳴る
- **rise** 動 昇る, 上がる
- **risen** 動 rise (昇る)の過去分詞
- **rising** 形 昇る, 高まる
- **river** 名 川
- **rock** 名 岩, 岸壁, 岩石
- **rocket** 名 打ち上げ花火
- **rode** 動 ride (乗る)の過去
- **roll** 動 ①転がる, 転がす ②(波などが)うねる, 横揺れする **roll up and down** (船が)上下に揺れる
- **roof** 名 屋根(のようなもの)
- **room** 名 部屋
- **rose** 名 ①バラ(の花) ②バラ色 動 rise (昇る)の過去
- **round** 副 ①回って **round and round** 周りにグルグルと 前 ①~を回って ②~の周囲に
- **row** 名 (横に並んだ)列 **in a row** 1列に(並んで), 連続して
- **run** 動 ①走る ②運行する ③(川が)流れる ④経営する **come running** 飛んでくる, かけつける **run about** 走り回る **run around** 走り回る **run away** 走り去る, 逃げ出す **run away from** ~から逃れる **run down** 走って行く, 追いかけて捕まえる, 追い詰める, 狩り出す **run into** (思いがけず)~に出会う, ~に駆け込む, ~の中に走って入る **run off** 走り去る, 逃げ去る **run on** ~を燃料とする, どんどん進む, 走り寄る **run through** 走り抜ける

- **rush** 動 突進する, せき立てる **rush in** ~に突入する, ~に駆けつける 名 突進, 突撃, 殺到 **a rush of air** 一陣の風
- **rushing noise [sound]** (サーッ, ザーッなどの)激しいノイズ[音]

S

- **sad** 形 ①悲しい, 悲しげな ②惨めな, 不運な
- **sadly** 副 悲しそうに, 不幸にも
- **sadness** 名 悲しみ, 悲哀
- **safe** 形 安全な, 危険のない
- **said** 動 say (言う)の過去, 過去分詞
- **sail** 名 帆 動 帆走する, 航海する
- **sailor** 名 船員, (ヨットの)乗組員
- **same** 形 ①同じ, 同様の ②前述の 代《the-》同一の人[物] 副《the-》同様に
- **sand** 名 ①砂 ②《-s》砂漠, 砂浜
- **sandbank** 名 砂州, 浅瀬
- **sang** 動 sing (歌う)の過去
- **sank** 動 sink (沈む)の過去
- **sat** 動 sit (座る)の過去, 過去分詞
- **save** 動 ①救う, 守る ②とっておく, 節約する
- **saw** 動 see (見る)の過去
- **say** 動 言う, 口に出す **say hello to** ~によろしく言う
- **scene** 名 光景, 風景
- **school** 名 学校
- **sea** 名 海
- **sea bottom** 名 海底
- **sea plant** 名 海産植物
- **Sea-folk** 名 人魚たち, 人魚の一族
- **Sea-King** 名 人魚の王
- **Sea-princess** 名 人魚の姫
- **sea-shore** 名 海岸, 海辺

WORD LIST

- **Sea-witch** 名 人魚の魔法使い
- **second** 形 第2の, 2番の
- **see** 動 ①見る, 見える, 見物する ②(～と)わかる, 認識する, 経験する ③会う ④考える, 確かめる, 調べる ⑤気をつける **Let me see.** ええと。 **see if** ～かどうかを確かめる **you see** あのね, いいですか
- **seem** 動 (～に)見える, (～のように)思われる
- **seen** 動 see (見る)の過去分詞
- **send** 動 ①送る, 届ける ②手紙を出す ③(人を～に)行かせる ④《～ + 人[物など] + ～ing》～を(ある状態に)する
- **sent** 動 send (送る)の過去, 過去分詞
- **set** 動 ①置く, 当てる, つける ②整える, 設定する ③(太陽・月などが)沈む ④(～を…の状態に)する, させる ⑤setの過去, 過去分詞 **set up** 配置する, セットする, 据え付ける
- **several** 形 ①いくつかの ②めいめいの
- **shade** 名 陰, 日陰
- **shake** 動 振る, 揺れる, 揺さぶる, 震える
- **shall** 助 ①《Iが主語で》～するだろう, ～だろう ②《I以外が主語で》(…に)～させよう, (…は)～することになるだろう **Shall I ～?** (私が)～しましょうか
- **share** 動 分配する, 共有する
- **sharp** 形 ①鋭い, とがった ②刺すような, きつい ③鋭敏な ④急な
- **she** 代 彼女は[が]
- **shell** 名 貝がら
- **shine** 動 ①光る, 輝く ②光らせる, 磨く
- **shining** 形 輝く, きらめく
- **shiny** 形 輝く, 光る
- **ship** 名 船
- **shoe** 名《-s》靴
- **shone** 動 shine (光る)の過去, 過去分詞
- **shook** 動 shake (振る)の過去
- **shore** 名 岸, 海岸, 陸 **on shore** 陸に, 上陸して
- **short** 形 短い
- **shorten** 動 短くする, 縮める
- **shortly** 副 まもなく, すぐに
- **shot** 動 shoot (撃つ)の過去, 過去分詞
- **should** 助 ～すべきである, ～したほうがよい
- **shoulder** 名 肩 動 肩にかつぐ
- **shout** 動 叫ぶ, 大声で言う, どなりつける
- **show** 動 ①見せる, 示す, 見える ②明らかにする, 教える **show off** 見せびらかす, 目立とうとする 名 表示, 見世物, ショー
- **shown** 動 show (見せる)の過去分詞
- **shy** 形 内気な, 恥ずかしがりの, 臆病な
- **sick** 形 ①病気の ②むかついて, いや気がさして
- **sickness** 名 病気
- **side** 名 側, 横, そば, 斜面
- **sight** 名 ①見ること, 視力, 視界 ②光景, 眺め
- **silk** 名 絹(布), 生糸 形 絹の, 絹製の
- **silver** 名 銀, 銀貨, 銀色 形 銀製の
- **silvery** 形 銀の, 銀で飾った
- **since** 接 ①～以来 ②～だから
- **sing** 動 ①(歌を)歌う ②さえずる
- **singing** 名 歌うこと, 歌声
- **single** 形 たった1つの
- **sink** 動 沈む, 沈める, 落ち込む
- **sister** 名 姉妹, 姉, 妹
- **sit** 動 ①座る, 腰掛ける ②止まる ③位置する **sit on** ～の上に乗る, ～の上に乗って動けないようにする **sit up** 起き上がる, 上半身を起こす

The Best of Andersen's Fairy Tales

- **six** 名6(の数字), 6人[個] 形6の, 6人[個]の
- **sixteen** 名16(の数字), 16人[個] 形16の, 16人[個]の
- **size** 名大きさ, 寸法, サイズ
- **skin** 名皮膚
- **skirt** 名スカート
- **sky** 名空, 天空, 大空
- **sleep** 動眠る, 寝る
- **slept** 動sleep(眠る)の過去, 過去分詞
- **small** 形小さい, 少ない
- **smart** 形利口な, 抜け目のない
- **smell** 動①(〜の)においがする ②においをかぐ 名①嗅覚 ②におい, 香り
- **smile** 動微笑する, にっこり笑う **smile at** 〜に微笑みかける
- **smoke** 名煙
- **snake** 名ヘビ(蛇)
- **snow** 名雪
- **snowy** 形雪の多い, 雪のように白い
- **so** 副①とても ②同様に, 〜もまた ③《先行する句・節の代用》そのように, そう **and so** そこで, それだから, それで **So be it.** それならそれでいい。 **so that** 〜するために, それで, 〜できるように **so ... that** 非常に〜なので… 接①だから, それで ②では, さて
- **soft** 形柔らかい
- **softly** 副柔らかに, 優しく, そっと
- **soil** 名土, 土地
- **sold** 動sell(売る)の過去, 過去分詞
- **soldier** 名兵士, 兵卒
- **some** 形①いくつかの, 多少の ②ある, 誰か, 何か 副約, およそ 代①いくつか ②ある人[物]たち
- **someone** 代ある人, 誰か
- **something** 代①ある物, 何か ②いくぶん, 多少

- **sometimes** 副時々, 時たま
- **song** 名歌, 詩歌, 鳴き声
- **Sonny** 名ソニー《名前》
- **soon** 副まもなく, すぐに, すみやかに
- **sort** 名種類, 品質 **a sort of** 〜のようなもの, 一種の
- **soul** 名①魂 ②精神, 心
- **sound** 名音, 騒音, 響き, サウンド 動①音がする, 鳴る ②(〜のように)思われる, (〜と)聞こえる **sound like** 〜のように聞こえる
- **space** 名空間, すき間, 余地, 場所, 間
- **Spain** 名スペイン《国名》
- **speak** 動話す, 言う, 演説する
- **speaking** 形話す, ものを言う
- **special** 形特別の, 特殊の
- **speechless** 形無言の, 口がきけない
- **spent** 動spend(使う)の過去, 過去分詞
- **spoke** 動speak(話す)の過去
- **spoken** 動speak(話す)の過去分詞
- **spoon** 名スプーン
- **spot** 名地点, 場所
- **spread** 動広がる, 広げる **spread out** 広げる, 展開する
- **springtime** 名春季, 春時間
- **stand** 動①立つ, 立たせる, 立っている, ある ②耐える, 立ち向かう **stand up** 立ち上がる
- **star** 名星 **evening star** 宵の明星, 金星
- **start** 動①出発する, 始まる, 始める ②生じる, 生じさせる **start doing** 〜し始める **start to do** 〜し始める
- **statue** 名像
- **stay** 動①とどまる, 泊まる, 滞在する ②持続する, (〜の)ままでいる **stay in** 家にいる, (場所)に泊まる,

WORD LIST

滞在する **stay up all night** 徹夜する

- □ **steadfast** 形 不変[不動]の, 忠実な
- □ **step** 名 歩み, 1歩
- □ **stick** 動 ①(突き)刺さる, 刺す ②くっつく, くっつける ③突き出る ④《受け身形で》いきづまる **stick out** 突き出す
- □ **still** 副 ①まだ, 今でも ②それでも(なお) 形 静止した, 静かな
- □ **stocking** 名 ストッキング, 長靴下
- □ **stone** 名 石, 小石
- □ **stood** 動 stand(立つ)の過去, 過去分詞
- □ **stop** 動 やめる, やめさせる, 止める, 止まる
- □ **storm** 名 嵐, 暴風雨
- □ **stormy** 形 ①嵐の, 暴風の ②激しい
- □ **story** 名 物語, 話
- □ **straight** 形 ①一直線の, まっすぐな, 直立[垂直]の ②率直な, 整然とした 副 ①一直線に, まっすぐに, 垂直に ②率直に
- □ **straighten** 動 まっすぐにする[なる]
- □ **strange** 形 ①知らない, 見[聞き]慣れない ②奇妙な, 変わった
- □ **strange-looking** 形 変な様子の, 奇妙な顔つきの
- □ **stranger** 名 見知らぬ人, 他人
- □ **stream** 名 小川, 流れ
- □ **street** 名 街路
- □ **strength** 名 力, 体力
- □ **strike** 動 打つ, ぶつかる
- □ **strong** 形 強い, 堅固な, 強烈な
- □ **struck** 動 strike(打つ)の過去, 過去分詞
- □ **stuck** 動 stick(刺さる, 突き出す)の過去, 過去分詞 **be stuck** いきづまる **become stuck** (異物が)詰まる
- □ **study** 動 勉強する

- □ **such** 形 ①そのような, このような ②そんなに, とても, 非常に **such a** そのような
- □ **suddenly** 副 突然, 急に
- □ **suffer** 動 ①(苦痛・損害などを)受ける, こうむる ②(病気に)なる, 苦しむ, 悩む
- □ **suit** 名 ①スーツ ②ひとそろい, 一組
- □ **summertime** 名 夏季, 夏時間
- □ **sun** 名 《the –》太陽, 日
- □ **sunk** 動 sink(沈む)の過去分詞
- □ **sunken** 形 沈んだ, 水中の, 地中の
- □ **sunken ship** 沈没船, 難破船
- □ **sunny** 形 ①日当たりのよい, 日のさす ②陽気な, 快活な
- □ **sunrise** 名 日の出
- □ **sunset** 名 日没, 夕焼け
- □ **sunshine** 名 日光
- □ **suppose** 動 ①仮定する, 推測する ②《be -d to》~することになっている, ~するものである
- □ **sure** 形 確かな, 確実な, 《be – to ~》必ず[きっと]~する, 確信して 副 確かに, まったく, 本当に **make sure** 確かめる, 確認する
- □ **surely** 副 確かに, きっと
- □ **surface** 名 ①表面, 水面 ②うわべ, 外見 **on the surface** 外面は, うわべは
- □ **surprised** 動 surprise(驚かす)の過去, 過去分詞 形 驚いた **be surprised at** ~に驚く
- □ **swam** 動 swim(泳ぐ)の過去
- □ **swan** 名 ハクチョウ(白鳥)
- □ **sweet** 形 ①甘い ②快い ③親切な ④かわいい, 魅力的な 名 ①《-s》甘い菓子 ②甘い味[香り], 甘いもの ③いとしい人, 《my -》あなた《呼びかけ》
- □ **sweetly** 副 甘く, 優しく
- □ **swim** 動 泳ぐ **swim out** 泳ぎ出る **swim up** 泳ぎ上る

- □ **sword** 名 剣, 刀
- □ **sword point** 剣先

T

- □ **table** 名 ①テーブル, 食卓, 台 ②一覧表
- □ **tail** 名 尾, しっぽ
- □ **take** 動 ①取る, 持つ ②持って[連れて]いく, 捕らえる ③乗る ④(時間・労力を)費やす, 必要とする ⑤(ある動作を)する ⑥飲む ⑦耐える, 受け入れる **take away** ①連れ去る ②取り上げる, 奪い去る ③取り除く **take care of** ～の世話をする, ～の面倒を見る, ～を管理する **take down** 下げる, 降ろす **take from** ～から引く, 選ぶ **take into** 手につかむ, 中に取り入れる **take off** (衣服を)脱ぐ, 取り去る, ～を取り除く, 離陸する, 出発する **take out of** ～から出す, ～に連れ出す **take someone away** (人)を連れ出す
- □ **taken** 動 take (取る)の過去分詞
- □ **talk** 動 話す, 語る, 相談する
- □ **tall** 形 高い, 背の高い
- □ **teach** 動 教える
- □ **tear** 名 涙
- □ **teeth** 名 tooth (歯)の複数
- □ **tell** 動 ①話す, 言う, 語る ②教える, 知らせる, 伝える ③わかる, 見分ける **tell ～ to …** ～に…するように言う
- □ **temple** 名 寺, 神殿
- □ **terrible** 形 恐ろしい, ひどい, ものすごい, つらい
- □ **than** 接 ～よりも, ～以上に
- □ **thank** 動 感謝する, 礼を言う **Thank God.** ありがたい
- □ **that** 形 その, あの 代 ①それ, あれ, その[あの]人[物] ②《関係代名詞》～である… 接 ～ということ, ～なので, ～だから 副 そんなに, それほど **after that** その後 **at that moment** その時に, その瞬間に **now that** 今や～だから, ～からには **so that** ～するために, それで, ～できるように **so ～ that …** 非常に～なので… **this and that** あれやこれや
- □ **the** 冠 ①その, あの《形容詞の前で》～な人々
- □ **their** 代 彼(女)らの, それらの
- □ **theirs** 代 彼(女)らのもの, それらのもの
- □ **them** 代 彼(女)らを[に], それらを[に]
- □ **then** 副 その時(に・は), それから, 次に **just then** そのとたんに
- □ **there** 副 ①そこに[で・の], そこへ, あそこへ ②《～ is [are] ～》～がある[いる] **down there** 下の方で[に] **get there** そこに到着する, 目的を達成する, 成功する **here and there** あちこちで **over there** あそこに **there lived ～.** ～が住んでいました。 **up there** あそこで
- □ **therefore** 副 したがって, それゆえ, その結果
- □ **these** 代 これら, これ 形 これらの, この
- □ **they** 代 ①彼(女)らは[が], それらは[が] ②(一般の)人々は[が]
- □ **thick** 形 厚い
- □ **thing** 名 ①物, 事 ②《-s》事情, 事柄 ③《one's -s》持ち物, 身の回り品 ④人, やつ
- □ **think** 動 思う, 考える **think highly of** ～を高く評価する, 尊敬する **think of** ～のことを考える, ～を思いつく, 考え出す
- □ **third** 名 第3(の人[物]) 形 第3の, 3番の
- □ **this** 形 ①この, こちらの, これを ②今の, 現在の **at this time** 現時点では, このとき **at this** これを見て, そこで(すぐに) **by this time** この時までに, もうすでに **like this** このような, こんなふうに **this and that** あれやこれや 代 ①これ, この人[物] ②今, ここ

WORD LIST

- **those** 形それらの, あれらの those who ～する人々 代それら[あれら]の人[物]
- **though** 接①～にもかかわらず, ～だが ②たとえ～でも as though あたかも～のように, まるで～みたいに 副しかし
- **thought** 動 think (思う) の過去, 過去分詞 名考え, 意見
- **thoughtful** 形思慮深い, 考え込んだ
- **thousand** 名①1000 (の数字), 1000人[個] ②《-s》何千, 多数 形①1000の, 1000人[個] の ②多数の
- **three** 名3 (の数字), 3人[個] 形3の, 3人[個]の
- **threw** 動 throw (投げる) の過去
- **through** 前～を通して, ～中を[に], ～中 副①通して ②終わりまで, まったく, すっかり
- **throw** 動投げる, 浴びせる, ひっかける throw a party パーティーを開く throw away ～を捨てる；～を無駄に費やす, 浪費する throw off 脱ぎ捨てる
- **thrown** 動 throw (投げる) の過去分詞
- **tie** 動結ぶ, 束縛する 名結び (目)
- **till** 前～まで (ずっと)
- **time** 名①時, 時間, 歳月 ②時期 ③期間 ④時代 ⑤回, 倍 at this time 現時点では, このとき by this time この時までに, もうすでに every time ～するときはいつも for the first time 初めて have a good time 楽しい時を過ごす in time 間に合って, やがて the last time この前～したとき
- **tin** 名錫 (すず), ブリキ
- **tired** 形①疲れた, くたびれた ②あきた, うんざりした
- **to** 前①《方向・変化》～へ, ～に, ～の方へ ②《程度・時間》～まで ③《適合・付加・所属》～に ④《-+動詞の原形》～するために[の], ～する, ～すること
- **toad** 名ヒキガエル
- **tobacco** 名たばこ
- **together** 副①一緒に, ともに ②同時に
- **told** 動 tell (話す) の過去, 過去分詞
- **tomorrow** 名明日 副明日は
- **tongue** 名舌
- **tonight** 名今夜, 今晩 副今夜は
- **too** 副①～も (また) ②あまりに～すぎる, とても～ too much 過度の too ～ to ……するには～すぎる
- **took** 動 take (取る) の過去
- **top** 名①頂上 ②ふた on top of ～の上(部)に
- **touch** 動①触れる, さわる, ～を触れさせる ②接触する ③感動させる 名①接触, 手ざわり ②手法 feel the touch of ～の接触を感じる
- **towards** 前①《運動の方向・位置》～の方へ, ～に向かって ②《目的》～のために
- **town** 名町, 都会, 都市
- **toy** 名おもちゃ
- **travel** 動旅行する
- **tree** 名木, 樹木
- **trouble** 名①困難, 迷惑 ②心配, 苦労 ③もめごと, 手ざわり get into trouble 面倒を起こす, 困った事になる, トラブルに巻き込まれる 動①悩ます, 心配させる ②迷惑をかける
- **troubled** 形不安げな
- **true** 形①本当の, 本物の, 真の ②誠実な, 確かな come true 実現する 副本当に, 心から
- **truly** 副本当に, 心から
- **truth** 名①真理, 事実, 本当 ②誠実, 忠実さ
- **try** 動試みる try out 実際に試してみる
- **tunnel** 名トンネル
- **turkey** 名七面鳥

- **turn** 動 ①ひっくり返す, 回転する[させる], 曲がる, 曲げる, 向かう, 向ける ②(〜に)なる, (〜に)変える **turn around** 振り向く, 向きを変える, 方向転換する **turn back** 元に戻る **turn down** (音量などを)小さくする, 弱くする, 拒絶する **turn in** 向きを変える, (向きを変えてわき道になどに)入る **turn on** 〜の方を向く **turn out** 外側に向く, ひっくり返す **turn to** 〜の方を向く 名 順番
- **turning water** 渦
- **twelve** 名 12(の数字), 12人[個] 形 12の, 12人[個]の
- **twenty-five** 名 25(の数字), 25人[個] 形 25の, 25人[個]の
- **twice** 副 2倍, 2度, 2回
- **two** 名 2(の数字), 2人[個] 形 2の, 2人[個]の
- **two-sided** 形 両面ある

U

- **ugh** 間 うえっ, げっ《嫌悪・恐怖を表す》, こんこん《せきの音》, ぶーぶー《不平を表す》
- **ugly** 形 ①醜い, ぶかっこうな ②いやな, 不快な, 険悪な
- **under** 前 ①《位置》〜の下[に] ②《状態》〜で, 〜を受けて, 〜のもと ③《数量》〜以下[未満]の, 〜より下の 副 下に[で], 従属[服従]して
- **underground** 形 地下の[にある]
- **understand** 動 理解する, わかる, 〜を聞いて知っている
- **undone** 動 undo(ほどく)の過去分詞 形 解かれた, ほどけた
- **unfit** 形 向いていない, 適さない
- **unhappily** 副 不幸に, 運悪く, 不愉快そうに
- **unhappy** 形 不運な, 不幸な
- **uniform** 名 制服
- **unkind** 形 不親切な, 意地の悪い
- **unknown** 形 知られていない, 不明の
- **unless** 接 もし〜でなければ, 〜しなければ
- **unseen** 形 目に見えない
- **until** 前 〜まで(ずっと) 接 〜の時まで, 〜するまで
- **unusual** 形 普通でない, 珍しい, 見[聞き]慣れない
- **up** 副 ①上へ, 上がって, 北へ ②立って, 行きついて ③向上して, 増して 前 ①〜の上(の方)へ, 高い方へ ②(道)に沿って **up and down** 上がったり下がったり, 行ったり来たり, あちこちと **up in the air** 空中に **up there** あそこで **up to** 〜まで, 〜に至るまで, 〜に匹敵して
- **upon** 前 ①《場所・接触》〜(の上)に ②《日・時》〜に ③《関係・従事》〜に関して, 〜について, 〜して 副 前へ, 続けて
- **upper** 形 上の, 上位の, 北方の **upper world** この世, 現世
- **us** 代 私たちを[に]
- **use** 動 ①使う, 用いる ②費やす 名 使用, 用途 **no use** 役に立たない, 用をなさない
- **used** 動 ①use(使う)の過去, 過去分詞 ②《 – to》よく〜したものだ, 以前は〜であった 形 ①慣れている,《get [become] – to》〜に慣れてくる ②使われた, 中古の
- **usually** 副 普通, いつも(は)

V

- **value** 名 価値, 値打ち, 価格
- **very** 副 とても, 非常に, まったく 形 本当の, きわめて, まさしくその
- **visit** 動 訪問する
- **visitor** 名 訪問客
- **voice** 名 声, 音声

WORD LIST

W

- **wait** 動 ①待つ,《 – for ~》~を待つ ②延ばす,延ばせる,遅らせる ③《 – on [upon] ~》~に仕える,給仕をする
- **waiting** 形 待っている
- **wake** 熟 wake up 起きる,目を覚ます
- **walk** 動 歩く,歩かせる,散歩する walk along (前へ)歩く,~に沿って歩く walk around 歩き回る,ぶらぶら歩く walk by 通りかかる walk on 歩き続ける walk right up まっすぐ歩いて上る walk to ~まで歩いて行く
- **walkway** 名 歩道
- **wall** 名 壁,塀
- **want** 動 ほしい,望む,~したい,~してほしい
- **warm** 形 暖かい,温暖な
- **warmly** 副 温かく,親切に
- **warmth** 名 暖かさ,思いやり
- **warrior** 名 戦士,軍人
- **was** 動《be の第1・第3人称単数現在 am, is の過去》~であった,(~に)いた[あった]
- **watch** 動 ①じっと見る,見物する ②注意[用心]する,監視する watch out for ~に注意する
- **water** 名 ①水 ②(川・湖・海などの)多量の水 turning water 渦
- **water plant** 水生植物
- **water-rat** 名 ウォーターラット,ミズネズミ
- **water-snake** 名 ミズヘビ
- **waterfall** 名 ①滝 ②どっと押し寄せるもの
- **waterway** 名 水路
- **wave** 名 波 wave after wave 次から次へと,次々に襲ってくる波 動 揺れる,揺らす,波立つ
- **way** 名 ①道,通り道 ②方向,距離 ③方法,手段 ④習慣 a long way off 遠く離れている,遠方にある long way はるかに on one's way out 出ていくときに way of the world 慣例,世の習わし way off 遠く離れて way out 出口,逃げ道
- **we** 代 私たちは[が]
- **wear** 動 着る,着ている,身につける
- **weather** 名 天気,天候,空模様
- **weave** 動 織る,編む
- **weaver** 名 織り手
- **weaving** 名 機織り
- **wedding** 名 結婚式,婚礼
- **week** 名 週,1週間
- **welcome** 動 歓迎する 形 歓迎される,自由に~してよい
- **well** 副 ①うまく,上手に ②十分に,よく,かなり as well なお,その上,同様に as well as ~と同様に be well -ed よく[十分に]~された 間 へえ,まあ,ええと
- **well-brought-up** 形 よく育った
- **well-dressed** 形 身なりのよい
- **went** 動 go (行く)の過去
- **were** 動《be の2人称単数・複数の過去》~であった,(~に)いた[あった]
- **whale** 名 クジラ(鯨)
- **what** 代 ①何が[を・に] ②《関係代名詞》~するところのもの[こと] 形 ①何の,どんな ②なんと ③~するだけの 副 いかに,どれほど
- **wheat** 名 小麦
- **when** 副 ①いつ ②《関係副詞》~するところの,~するとその時,~するとき 接 ~の時,~するとき 代 いつ
- **whenever** 接 ①~するときはいつでも,~するたびに ②いつ~しても
- **where** 副 ①どこに[で] ②《関係副詞》~するところの,そしてそこで,~するところ 接 ~なところに[へ],~するところに[へ] 代 ①どこ,どの

点 ②〜するところの
- **wherever** 接 どこでも、どこへ[で]〜するとも 副 いったいどこへ[に・で]
- **which** 形 ①どちらの、どの、どれでも ②どんな〜でも、そしてこの 代 ①どちら、どれ、どの人[物] ②《関係代名詞》〜するところの
- **while** 接 ①〜の間(に)、〜する間(に) ②一方、〜なのに 名 しばらくの間、一定の時
- **white** 形 ①白い、(顔色などが)青ざめた ②白人の 名 白、白色
- **white marble** 白大理石
- **who** 代 ①誰が[は]、どの人 ②《関係代名詞》〜するところの(人) **those who** 〜する人々
- **whole** 形 全体の、すべての、完全な、満〜、丸〜 名《the –》全体、全部
- **whom** 代 ①誰を[に] ②《関係代名詞》〜するところの人、そしてその人を
- **why** 副 ①なぜ、どうして ②《関係副詞》〜するところの(理由) 間 ①おや、まあ ②もちろん、なんだって ③ええと
- **wide** 形 幅の広い、広範囲の、幅が〜ある 副 広く、大きく開いて
- **wife** 名 妻、夫人
- **wild** 形 ①野生の ②荒涼として ③荒っぽい ④奇抜な
- **wildly** 副 荒々しく、乱暴に、むやみに
- **will** 助 〜だろう、〜しよう、する(つもりだ)
- **willow** 名 ヤナギ(柳)
- **win** 動 勝つ、獲得する、達する
- **wind** 名 風
- **window** 名 窓、窓ガラス
- **wing** 名 翼、羽
- **winter** 名 冬
- **wise** 形 賢明な、聡明な、博学の
- **wish** 動 望む、願う、(〜であればいいと)思う **I wish 〜 were** … 私が〜なら …なのに。《仮定法過去》
- **witch** 名 魔法使い、魔女
- **with** 前 ①《同伴・付随・所属》〜と一緒に、〜を身につけて、〜とともに ②《様態》〜(の状態)で、〜して ③《手段・道具》〜で、〜を使って
- **without** 前 〜なしで、〜がなく、〜しないで
- **woke** 動 wake (目が覚める)の過去
- **woman** 名 (成人した)女性、婦人
- **won't** will notの短縮形
- **wonder** 動 ①不思議に思う、(〜に)驚く ②(〜かしらと)思う
- **wonderful** 形 驚くべき、すばらしい、すてきな
- **wondrous** 形 驚くべき、すばらしい
- **wood** 名 ①《しばしば-s》森、林 ②木材、まき
- **wooden** 形 木製の、木でできた
- **wooden shoe** 木ぐつ
- **word** 名 ①語、単語 ②ひと言 ③《one's –》約束
- **wore** 動 wear (着ている)の過去
- **work** 動 働く、勉強する、取り組む **work on** 〜で働く、〜に取り組む、〜を説得する、〜に効く 名 仕事
- **world** 名《the –》世界、〜界 **in the world** 世界で **upper world** この世、現世 **way of the world** 慣例、世の習わし
- **worry** 動 悩む、悩ませる、心配する[させる] **worry about** 〜のことを心配する
- **worse** 形 いっそう悪い、より劣った、よりひどい
- **would** 助《willの過去》①〜するだろう、〜するつもりだ ②〜したものだ **would have** … **if 〜** もし〜だったとしたら…しただろう **would like to** 〜したいと思う **would rather** 〜する方がよい

WORD LIST

- □ **wrong** 形 ①間違った,(道徳上)悪い ②調子が悪い,故障した **be wrong with** (〜にとって)よくない,〜が故障している
- □ **wrote** 動 write (書く)の過去

Y

- □ **yard** 名 庭,構内
- □ **year** 名 ①年,1年 ②〜歳 **for 〜 years** 〜年間,〜年にわたって
- □ **years old** 〜歳の
- □ **yellow** 形 黄色の 名 黄色
- □ **yes** 副 はい,そうです
- □ **yet** 副 ①《否定文で》まだ〜(ない[しない]) ②《疑問文で》もう ③《肯定文で》まだ,今もなお **and yet** それなのに,それにもかかわらず **not yet** まだ〜してない 接 それにもかかわらず,しかし,けれども **Yet his wife she must become** しかしそれでも彼の妻に彼女はならなければならない
- □ **you** 代 ①あなた(方)は[が],あなた(方)を[に] ②(一般に)人は **you see** あのね,いいですか
- □ **young** 形 若い,幼い,青年の
- □ **your** 代 あなた(方)の
- □ **yours** 代 あなた(方)のもの
- □ **yourself** 代 あなた自身

ラダーシリーズ
The Best of Andersen's Fairy Tales
アンデルセン名作選

2012年4月5日　第1刷発行

著　者　ハンス・クリスチャン・アンデルセン

発行者　浦　晋亮

発行所　IBCパブリッシング株式会社
　　　　〒162-0804 東京都新宿区中里町29番3号
　　　　菱秀神楽坂ビル9F
　　　　Tel. 03-3513-4511　Fax. 03-3513-4512
　　　　www.ibcpub.co.jp

© IBC Publishing, Inc. 2012

印刷　シナノ印刷株式会社
装丁　伊藤 理恵　　本文イラスト　杉山 薫里
組版データ　ITC Berkeley Oldstyle Pro Medium+Cochin Bold

落丁本・乱丁本は、小社宛にお送りください。送料小社負担にてお取り替えいたします。
本書の無断複写（コピー）は著作権法上での例外を除き禁じられています。

Printed in Japan
ISBN 978-4-7946-0137-7

カバーイラスト：『人魚姫』（*Arthur Edmund Dulac, 1837, Wikipedia*）

※本書はラダーシリーズ『アンデルセン珠玉童話選 (Andersen's Fairy Tales)』と
　『アンデルセン・クラシックス (Andersen's Classic Stories)』を元に再構成したものです。